Social Studies Alive!®
Regions of Our Country

WITHDRAWN

Please Note: TCI uses the terms visual and transparency interchangeably in this lesson guide. You will
find the visuals for this program on the Web at
Teachtci.com or in the bound book of visuals.

Chief Executive Officer: Bert Bower

Chief Operating Officer: Amy Larson

Director of Product Development: Liz Russell

Managing Editor: Laura Alavosus

Editorial Project Manager: Lara Fox

Project Editors: Wendy Frey and Nancy O'Leary

Editorial Associates: Anna Embree and Sarah Sudano

Production Manager: Lynn Sanchez

Design Manager: Jeff Kelly

Graphic Designer: Victoria Philp

Photo Edit Manager: Margee Robinson

Photo Editor: Diane Austin

Art Editors: Eric Houts and Sarah Wildfang

Audio Manager: Katy Haun

TCi™   Teachers' Curriculum Institute
P.O. Box 50996
Palo Alto, CA 94303

Customer Service: 800-497-6138
www.teachtci.com

ISBN 978-1-58371-854-4
3 4 5 6 7 8 9 10 -MLI- 15 14 13 12 11 10

Acknowledgements

Program Director

Bert Bower

Program Consultant

Vicki LaBoskey, Ph.D., Professor of Education, Mills College, Oakland, California

Student Edition Writers

Susan Buckley

Diane Hanover

Diane Hart

Peter Lacey

Curriculum Developers

Joyce Bartky

Anne Maloney

Elizabeth Sarica

Steve Seely

Kelly Shafksy

Reading Specialist

Barbara Schubert, Ph.D., Reading Specialist, Saint Mary's College, Moraga, California

Teacher and Content Consultants

Lynn Casey, Teacher, Husmann Elementary School, Crystal Lake, Illinois

Jane Crowe, Teacher, Brookwood Elementary School, Tuscaloosa County, Alabama

Khieta Davis, Teacher, Flower City School #54, Rochester, New York

Ann Dawson, Educational Consultant, Intermediate Curriculum Specialist, Gahanna, Ohio

Shirley Jacobs, Library Media Specialist, Irving Elementary School, Bloomington, Illinois

Elizabeth McKenna, Teacher, St. Thomas Aquinas Catholic School, Diocese of Orlando, Florida

Mitch Pascal, Social Studies Specialist, Arlington County Schools, Arlington, Virginia

Becky Suthers, Retired Teacher, Stephen F. Austin Elementary, Weatherford, Texas

Tiffany Wilson, Teacher, Corbell Elementary, Frisco, Texas

Literature Consultant

Regina M. Rees, Ph.D., Assistant Professor, Beeghly College of Education, Youngstown State University, Youngstown, Ohio

Music Specialist

Beth Yankee, Teacher, The Woodward School for Technology and Research, Kalamazoo, Michigan

Maps

Mapping Specialists, Ltd., Madison, Wisconsin

How to Use This Program   ix

Chapter 1   **Discovering the Social Sciences**   1

Students learn why the study of the social sciences is important to understanding human behavior. In a Response Group activity, they discuss artifacts from the perspective of each of these social science traditions: economics, geography, political science, and history.

Chapter 2   **Exploring Regions of the United States**   11

Students apply basic map skills to learn about the regions of the United States. In a Social Studies Skill Builder, they interpret a series of special purpose maps depicting five regions of the United States and attempt to identify the locations where five images of the United States were taken.

Chapter 3   **The Peopling of the United States**   25

Students learn how five ethnic groups—American Indians, Latinos, European Americans, African Americans, and Asian Americans—came to this country and contributed to its growth and development. In a Social Studies Skill Builder, they work in pairs to read about one of the groups and draw images and symbols to represent that group's experience.

Chapter 4   **A Train Tour of the Northeast**   37

Students take a "train tour" to learn about the Northeast region of the United States. In a Writing for Understanding activity, groups of students sit on a "train" and listen to a tour guide while they view images of places in the Northeast. Through interactive experiences, they learn key concepts and facts about the Northeast. Then they write a letter describing what they have seen on their tour.

Contents

Chapter 5 **Population Density and Life in the Northeast** **51**

Students learn how population density in the Northeast affects the lives of the people who live there. In an Experiential Exercise, students use their bodies and desks to simulate the population density of the Northeast and several comparative locales. They respond to a series of questions about how population density might affect people's lives. Then, they read and record notes about how life in the Northeast megalopolis differs from life in a small town.

Chapter 6 **A Boat and Bus Tour of the Southeast** **63**

Students tour the Southeast region of the United States by boat and bus. In a Writing for Understanding activity, students listen to a tour guide and view images depicting life in the Southeast. The tour stops at three sites, where students engage in interactive experiences and learn key concepts and facts about the region. Then, they write a letter about their excursions in the Southeast.

Chapter 7 **The Effects of Geography on Life in the Southeast** **77**

Students learn how geography affects life in the Southeast region. In a Social Studies Skill Builder, students look at maps and answer questions about climate, elevation, natural resources, and bodies of water. Then, they hypothesize and read about the effects of geography on life in the Southeast.

Chapter 8 **A Crop Duster Tour of the Midwest** **91**

Students tour the Midwest region of the United States. In a Writing for Understanding activity, they listen to a tour guide and view images of the Midwest. Through interactive experiences, students learn key concepts and facts about the region. Then, they use their notes to write a letter about their excursions in the Midwest.

Chapter 9 **Agricultural Changes in the Midwest** **105**

Students learn how agriculture in the Midwest changed from 1800 to today. In a Visual Discovery activity, they analyze images of farm life in 1800, 1900, and today. Then they create act-it-outs to demonstrate their understanding of farm life during these periods.

Chapter 10 A Big Rig Tour of the Southwest **121**

Students take a "big rig tour" of the Southwest region of the United States. In a Writing for Understanding activity, they sit in "big rigs" in groups of three, listen to a tour guide, and view nine images depicting life in the Southwest. The trucks stop at three sites, where students learn more through interactive experiences.

Chapter 11 A Case Study in Water Use: The Colorado River **134**

Students explore the history of how people have used and shared the water of the Colorado River. In an Experiential Exercise, they act out the roles of people living near the Colorado River in four different time periods to understand how its water has been used and shared, and how it might be used in the future.

Chapter 12 A Van and Airplane Tour of the West **149**

Students take a "van and airplane tour" of the West region of the United States. In a Writing for Understanding activity, they listen to a tour guide and view nine images of places in the West. The tour stops at three sites, where students learn more through interactive experiences that teach key concepts of the chapter. Then, they use their notes to write a letter about their excursions in the West.

Chapter 13 Cities of the West **161**

Students learn about seven cities in the West. In a Problem Solving Groupwork activity, they research, plan, and perform television commercials about cities in the West.

Chapter 14 Researching Your State's Geography **171**

Students research the geography of their state using maps, atlases, library books, and the Internet. In a Social Studies Skill Builder, pairs of students design a board game that includes the geographic features they identified. Afterward, they take turns playing each other's board games to test their geographic knowledge of the state.

Contents

Chapter 15 Researching Your State's History   **181**

Students learn how to investigate their state's history. In a
Writing for Understanding activity, they research a building, create a model of the building, write a script that tells
about one era in the state's history from the perspective of
the building, and bring the building to life to tell the story
of their state's history.

Chapter 16 Researching Your State's Economy   **193**

Students learn the fundamentals of their state's economy.
In a Problem Solving Groupwork activity, they work in
groups to research one of eight economic activities and
then create a museum exhibit about that activity. Each
figure in the exhibit "comes to life" to talk about the
essential aspects of the state's economy.

Chapter 17 Researching Your State's Government   **205**

Students learn about their state's government. In a
Writing for Understanding activity, they play a game to
learn the sequence of a state's legislative process. After
researching their state's government, they write a letter
to a state leader asking that he or she help solve a problem
by working to get a new law passed.

Analysis of Skills in Grade 4   **212**
Credits   **215**

How to Use This Program:
Social Studies Alive!
Regions of Our Country

Teaching with the TCI Approach means shifting to a student-centered, activity-based classroom. To meet this exciting challenge, this introduction to the Lesson Guide for *Social Studies Alive! Regions of Our Country* will give you the basics you need to start teaching this program with confidence right away.

The TCI Approach   x

Multiple Intelligences Teaching Strategies   xii

Program Components   xiv

Walking Through a Lesson   xvi

Organizing a TCI Classroom   xviii

Creating a Cooperative, Tolerant Classroom   xix

Using the Interactive Student Notebook   xx

Integrating Reading Language Arts   xxii

Assessing Learning   xxiv

Enhancing Instruction with TeachTCI   xxvi

Growing Professionally   xxviii

Letter to Families   xxix

The TCI Approach

Why is the TCI Approach so effective at igniting students' passion for learning? The TCI Approach consists of a series of instructional practices that allow students of all abilities to experience key social studies concepts. It has eight important features.

Theory- and Research-Based Active Instruction

Lessons and activities are based on five well-established theories.

Understanding by Design　Grant Wiggins and Jay McTighe maintain that teaching for deep understanding must begin with planning the big ideas students should learn. That's why you will see an Essential Question at the start of every chapter in *Social Studies Alive! Regions of Our Country*.

Nonlinguistic Representation　Research by Robert Marzano and colleagues demonstrates that teaching with nonlinguistic activities helps improve comprehension. Use of movement and graphic note-taking are both key to TCI lessons.

Multiple Intelligences　Howard Gardner believes that all students are intelligent—just not in the same ways. TCI activities address seven of Gardner's intelligences: verbal-linguistic, logical-mathematical, visual-spatial, bodily-kinesthetic, musical-rhythmic, interpersonal, and intrapersonal.

Cooperative Interaction　Elizabeth Cohen's research shows that cooperative groupwork leads to learning gains and higher student achievement. Working in small groups is a cornerstone of TCI activities.

Spiral Curriculum　Jerome Bruner championed the idea of the spiral curriculum, in which students learn progressively—understanding more difficult concepts through a process of step-by-step discovery. TCI questioning strategies spiral from simple recall to higher-order thinking skills such as analysis and evaluation.

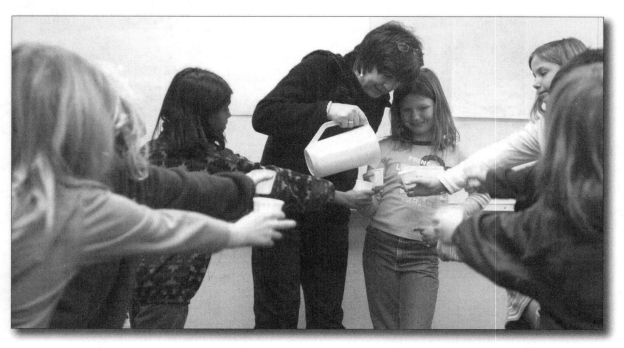

Standards-Based Content

Dynamic lessons that integrate hands-on learning and content reading build mastery of state and national standards in both social studies and language arts.

Preview Assignment

Short, engaging exercises at the start of each lesson help you preview key concepts and engage students' knowledge and personal experience. In *Social Studies Alive! Regions of Our Country,* each Preview includes Connecting to Prior Knowledge, Developing Vocabulary, and Building Background Knowledge.

Multiple Intelligences Teaching Strategies

TCI activities incorporate six multiple intelligences teaching strategies:

- Visual Discovery
- Social Studies Skill Builder
- Experiential Exercise
- Writing for Understanding
- Response Group
- Problem Solving Groupwork

These six strategies are explained in detail on the following pages.

Considerate Text

Carefully structured reading materials enable students at all levels to understand what they read. Uncluttered pages present content in digestible "chunks." Engaging images reinforce content, while consistent vocabulary development improves student comprehension.

Graphically Organized Reading Notes

Visually engaging Reading Notes help students record key ideas and make meaning out of what they read. By combining graphic and written work, students improve their comprehension and retention of content.

Processing Assignment

An end-of-lesson assignment involving multiple intelligences and higher-order thinking skills challenges students to apply what they have learned in a variety of creative ways.

Assessments to Inform Instruction

Carefully designed chapter tests move students through a progression of thinking skills, from comprehension to skills application to critical thinking. Test results in these three areas show you where students are succeeding and where they need more instruction.

Multiple Intelligences Teaching Strategies

The TCI Approach uses the six teaching strategies described here to bring learning alive. All six strategies appear in the *Social Studies Alive! Regions of Our Country* Lesson Guide with detailed, step-by-step instructions. Support materials for each chapter's activities appear in the *Lesson Masters,* Transparencies, and Placards as well as on the *Sounds of Social Studies* CD and TeachTCI CD-ROM.

Visual Discovery

In Visual Discovery activities, students view, touch, interpret, and bring to life compelling images as they discover key social studies concepts. Seeing and interacting with an image in combination with reading and recording notes helps students remember important content.

Here are some tips for Visual Discovery activities:

- Arrange your classroom so that projected images will be large and clear.
- Ask carefully sequenced questions that lead to discovery.
- Challenge students to read about each image and apply what they learn.
- Have students interact with each image to demonstrate learning.

Social Studies Skill Builder

In Social Studies Skill Builders, students work in pairs or small groups on fast-paced, skill-oriented tasks such as reading maps, categorizing information, analyzing artifacts and primary sources, and comparing and contrasting ideas to enhance their understanding of chapter content.

Here are some tips for Social Studies Skill Builders:

- Teach each skill through modeling and guided practice.
- Prepare students to work in pairs or small groups.
- Set clear expectations, allow students to practice each skill repeatedly, and give immediate feedback.
- Debrief the activity to help students make connections to key social studies concepts.

Experiential Exercise

In Experiential Exercises, participating in short, memorable experiences helps students grasp social studies concepts. Through the use of movement and introspection, students capture a moment or feeling that is central to understanding a particular concept or historical event.

Here are some tips for Experiential Exercises:

- Prepare students for a safe, successful experience by arranging the classroom appropriately, communicating clear behavioral and learning expectations, giving clear directions, anticipating student reactions, and recognizing teachable moments.

- Bring authenticity to the experience by assuming an appropriate persona, hamming it up, and using simple props, costumes, music, and sound effects.
- Allow students to express their feelings immediately after the experience.
- Ask carefully sequenced questions to help students make connections between their experience and key concepts or events.

Writing for Understanding

Writing for Understanding activities begin with a rich experience—such as viewing powerful images, role-playing, discussing complex issues, or acting out key events—to write about. Students develop ideas and form opinions during the experience, before starting to write. The experience becomes a springboard for writing, challenging students to clarify ideas, organize information, and express what they have learned.

Here are some tips for Writing for Understanding activities:

- Have students record their ideas, thoughts, and feelings in prewriting activities.
- Guide students through the writing process.
- Use peer feedback groups as part of the revision process.

Response Group

In Response Group activities, students work in small groups with thought-provoking resources to discuss critical thinking questions among themselves. A presenter then shares each group's findings with the class.

Here are some tips for Response Group activities:

- Create mixed-ability groups and a suitable classroom arrangement.
- Prepare students to answer provocative critical thinking questions.
- Allow groups time to prepare their responses.
- Facilitate a lively class discussion.

Problem Solving Groupwork

In Problem Solving Groupwork activities, students work in heterogeneous groups to create projects that require multiple abilities so that every student can contribute. Within a group, each student takes a defined role. After completing their task, groups present their projects to the class.

Here are some tips for Problem Solving Groupwork activities:

- Review ground rules for working cooperatively in groups.
- Give group members clearly defined roles and requirements.
- Give groups autonomy and time to prepare high-quality projects.
- Allow groups to showcase their work.

Program Components

The components of *Social Studies Alive! Regions of Our Country* work together to maximize your time and creativity. Everything you need to provide insightful and stimulating classroom experiences is included in the program. There are also plenty of opportunities to add your own resources.

Student Edition

Each chapter poses an Essential Question to help students focus their learning on key concepts. In the Student Edition you will find

- 17 chapters that introduce basic social studies concepts such as "Exploring Regions of the United States," "The Peopling of the United States," and "Researching Your State's Economy."

- considerate text that is uncluttered and easy to navigate.

- graphic elements that spark student interest and foster comprehension.

- highlighted social studies vocabulary terms.

- a high-interest Reading Further case study at the end of each chapter that explores dimensions of the chapter's concepts in depth.

Lesson Guide

"Command Central" for the program, with detailed, step-by-step instructions for each chapter, as well as the following resources to help you plan your lesson:

- a materials list and estimated timing

- both social studies and language arts objectives

- a planning guide for pacing the lesson

- language arts sidebars at point of use to help integrate vocabulary development, reading strategies, writing tips, and speaking and listening into social studies instruction

- suggestions for differentiating instruction for English language learners, students with special needs, and enrichment

- a Guide to Reading Notes and a Guide to Reading Further—answers to objective questions that appear in the Interactive Student Notebook

- suggestions for enhancing learning with online resources and literature connections

- answers for assessments

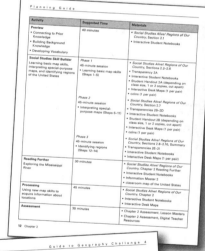

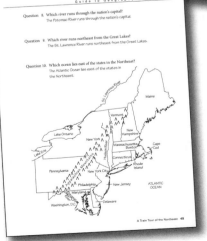

Lesson Masters

Reproducible pages for classroom support, identified in the materials list for each chapter in the Lesson Guide, including

- Student Handouts and Information Masters
- chapter assessments

Interactive Student Notebook

Each student's personal repository of learning, all in one place. For each chapter, the Interactive Student Notebook includes

- a Preview assignment
- graphically organized Reading Notes
- one or more activity pages to support the Reading Further in the Student Edition
- a Processing assignment

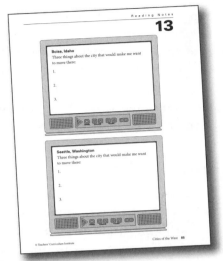

Transparencies and Placards

Visual support for chapter activities, including maps, photographs, and illustrations

Sounds of Social Studies CD

Audio tracks of songs, dramatizations, and sound effects that play an essential role in several lessons

Solutions for Effective Instruction

A rich collection of classroom-tested strategies for enriching your teaching through

- integrating reading/language arts
- differentiating instruction
- building social studies/critical thinking skills

Interactive Desk Map

Durable two-sided map to help students improve their geographic knowledge and skills. The Lesson Guide provides specific suggestions for using each map.

TeachTCI

The "home base" for TCI lessons—everything you need for planning and instruction. Includes a CD-ROM with a link to exclusive resources at www.teachtci.com. TeachTCI gives you

- all the materials in the Teacher Resources kit in digital format
- Assessment Creator
- Enrichment Resources
- lesson tips from the TCI community
- customized state correlations

Walking Through a Lesson

While students look forward to the wide variety of activities they will experience in a TCI classroom, they also reap the benefits of TCI's consistent organization of learning in the chapters. Following sound pedagogical practices, each lesson begins with a Preview assignment to spark interest and connect to prior knowledge, progresses through a dynamic class activity and visually engaging Reading Notes, then moves to Reading Further, and concludes with a Processing assignment that asks students to apply what they have learned.

Preview

The Preview assignment is a short, engaging task that foreshadows upcoming content. The goal is to ignite interest, activate prior knowledge, tap a wide range of intelligences, and prepare students to tackle new concepts. The Preview is built around three essentials for frontloading a lesson: Connecting to Prior Knowledge, Developing Vocabulary, and Building Background Knowledge. In *Social Studies Alive! Regions of Our Country,* students complete the Preview assignment in their Interactive Student Notebooks.

Types of Preview assignments include

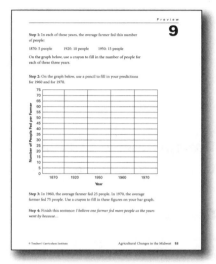

- recalling personal experiences and emotions
- comparing personal experience with key concepts
- creating maps, drawings, and diagrams based on existing knowledge
- responding to images, songs, and spoken text
- making predictions

Classroom Activity

At the heart of each TCI lesson is the classroom activity that engages students in social studies content and concepts through hands-on learning experiences. These core activities use the six TCI teaching strategies.

Examples of classroom activities in *Social Studies Alive! Regions of Our Country* include

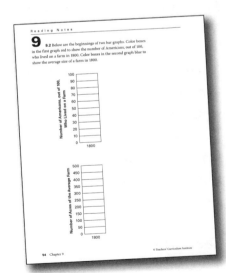

- Visual Discovery: Agricultural Changes in the Midwest
- Social Studies Skill Builder: The Effects of Geography on Life in the Southeast
- Experiential Exercise: A Case Study in Water Use: The Colorado River
- Writing for Understanding: A Train Tour of the Northeast
- Response Group: Discovering the Social Sciences
- Problem Solving Groupwork: Cities of the West

Reading Notes

One of the most powerful ways to improve students' comprehension and retention is to have them complete graphic Reading Notes for each chapter. When students record information in engaging, visual ways, they are better able to recall social studies content months, and even years, later. Students complete the Reading Notes in their Interactive Student Notebooks.

Types of Reading Notes include

- maps
- T-charts
- commemorative plaques
- television commercials
- annotated drawings
- letters

Reading Further

To support the Reading Further in every chapter of the Student Edition, students complete a page in their Interactive Student Notebooks.

Types of Reading Further activities include

- newspaper articles
- timelines
- sensory figures
- proclamations

Processing

Processing assignments are wrap-up activities that challenge students to synthesize the information in a chapter to demonstrate their understanding. The intent is to allow students to apply what they have learned actively so that you—and they—can assess their comprehension. Students complete the Processing assignment in their Interactive Student Notebooks.

Types of Processing assignments include

- annotated maps
- interviews
- research reports
- posters
- journal entries

Organizing a TCI Classroom

Most of the *Social Studies Alive! Regions of Our Country* activities require students to move into small groups of two, three, or four. With a brief training exercise, you can teach students how to form groups quickly without wasting valuable time.

Moving Your Classroom Furniture

Tell students that they will be working in small groups of different sizes throughout the year. They must know how to move into each grouping quickly and efficiently, with all their materials. When working in pairs, they should place their desks either side by side or face to face, with the edges touching. For groups of three or more, the front corners of the desks must touch.

With these expectations clear, allow students to practice moving into groups. Randomly assign students to groups and indicate where they should meet. Then say "Go!" and time them. If necessary, allow the class to discuss what went wrong and brainstorm ideas for getting into groups more efficiently. Have students repeat the process until they can do it in "record time."

If you spend time at the beginning of the school year teaching this skill, you will save hours of instructional time. Your goal should be for students to be able to form various group configurations in less than one minute, without your needing to touch any student furniture.

Organizing Your Teacher Resources

Social Studies Alive! Regions of Our Country comes with all the materials you need to excite your students. It will be up to you, however, to gather the materials for each chapter and organize them in a way that makes it fast and easy to conduct activities year after year. Here are some tips to save you time and make running your classroom much easier:

- Begin preparation for each activity by gathering everything on the materials list, such as Placards, Transparencies, and the *Sounds of Social Studies* CD. Consider opening the Lesson Guide and *Lesson Masters* files on the *TeachTCI* CD-ROM and printing out all pages of both.

- Make all the copies you will need of *Lesson Masters,* such as assessments, Student Handouts, and Information Masters.

- When you finish each activity, place all the printed materials in a clear, resealable plastic bag (an ideal size is 10 by 12 inches) with the Lesson Guide on top as a "label." This will keep the many individual activity pieces together and will ensure that next year's preparation takes virtually no time.

Creating a Cooperative, Tolerant Classroom

The interactive, experiential, and stimulating learning at the heart of the TCI Approach can happen only when students feel comfortable sharing ideas, taking risks, working cooperatively, tolerating differences, and disagreeing honestly and respectfully with you and their classmates. Thus, you need to take purposeful steps to develop a "safe" community in your classroom. Here are some tips for creating a cooperative, tolerant classroom:

- Greet your students at the door every day to make a personal connection with them as they enter your classroom.
- Explain your expectations for classroom behavior, using specific examples. You may also involve students in shaping class rules.
- Convince students that learning to work effectively with others will benefit them throughout their lives.
- Teach students how to move efficiently into groups of various sizes.
- Use role-playing activities to teach students cooperative skills.
- Form mixed-ability groups.

You may wish to make a poster of these reminders for your classroom:

How to Work Cooperatively in Groups

1. Smile, be friendly, and introduce yourself.
2. Sit properly.
3. Look at the person talking.
4. Listen.
5. Take turns.
6. Be helpful and nice.
7. Work out problems on your own.
8. Follow directions and stay on task.

Using the Interactive Student Notebook

In the Interactive Student Notebook, all parts of the integrated lesson come together as students create a dynamic record of their learning. Unlike traditional worksheets, the activities in the notebook reach out to students, inviting them to be active participants in their own learning. The notebook encourages students to use a variety of intelligences, not just linguistic intelligence. Especially important for the primary grades, the notebook helps students to organize systematically as they learn. Over the course of the school year, the notebook becomes a portfolio of individual learning. Teachers, students, and even family members can review a student's progress in writing, thinking, and organization skills. This makes the notebook a valuable tool for parent conferences.

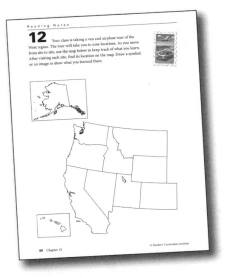

Hints for Making Effective Interactive Student Notebooks

Teachers use the Interactive Student Notebook in a variety of forms. Some give their students the consumable notebook that is provided with TCI's core program materials. Teachers who elect to use this consumable can follow the sequence exactly as designed, having students complete the specified Previews, Reading Notes, Reading Furthers, and Processing assignments. This system is helpful to teachers who are new to the TCI Approach, since they can rely on the published Interactive Student Notebook for support while they are learning to use the essential elements and strategies of the program.

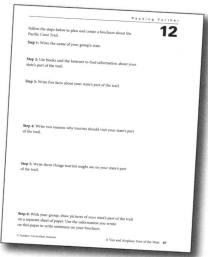

Other teachers elect to supplement the printed notebook with their own handouts and materials that students bring to school. You will notice that the Interactive Student Notebook is punched and perforated to give you flexibility in how you use it. You may wish to have students use spiral-bound notebooks, clasp folders, or three-ring binders to combine the materials, cutting and pasting as they create their own unique Interactive Student Notebooks. In this format, the TCI materials serve as the backbone, but teachers have the flexibility to tailor instruction to suit their needs.

Regardless of the format you plan to use, the following hints will increase the effectiveness of your Interactive Student Notebooks and allow students' individual styles to flourish:

- Supply materials that inspire creativity. An abundance of materials—colored pencils and markers, scissors, glue sticks, colored highlighters—will spark creativity for notebook assignments.

- Let students create their own covers. Encourage students to create a colorful cover that reflects what they are learning. This immediately sends the message that the notebooks will be their own creations that they can take pride in, and it helps cut down on the number of lost notebooks during the year.

- Personalize the notebooks with an author page. Have each student create a page about himself or herself to include at the front of the notebook. With both a personalized cover and an author page, very few notebooks will get lost.

- Establish clear guidelines for student work. Decide ahead of time what you expect your students to produce in their notebooks, and clearly communicate your expectations. It will be helpful to model neatness and accuracy for students, particularly in the beginning of the year.

Managing Assessment of Interactive Student Notebooks

Because so much of students' work appears in these notebooks, you will need an efficient and accurate system for assessing them.

Informal Assessment Monitor student notebooks aggressively in the first few weeks of school. Look at notebooks as you walk around, making positive comments and helpful suggestions. Here are some additional ideas:

- While students work on another assignment, conduct a quick review of the previous night's homework, giving students checks or special stamps to denote completed assignments.

- Provide a model of outstanding work for an assignment or set of class notes.

- Allow students to use their notebooks on a quiz or test. This will come as a pleasant surprise and reward for students with well-organized notebooks.

Formal Assessment At the beginning of the year, clearly explain the criteria on which you will evaluate notebooks, such as quality and completeness of assignments, visual appearance, neatness, higher-order thinking, and organization. Here are some additional ideas for assessing student work:

- Create a simple rubric that identifies the criteria you feel are most important. Post it in your classroom.

- Stagger notebook collection so that you correct only one portion of the class at a time.

- Grade selectively. Don't feel compelled to grade every notebook entry.

- Have students assess their own work. This process enables them to reflect on their learning and critically review their progress. Explain that if your assessment differs markedly from theirs—better or worse—they will have the opportunity to discuss the reasons for your assessment.

Integrating Reading Language Arts

In recent years, many elementary teachers have found it hard to find time for social studies. With greater emphasis on reading instruction, writing, and math, there seems to be less time to fit in any history, geography, civics, or economics. Yet these subjects are essential to the development of young minds and responsible citizens in our democracy.

Social Studies Alive! Regions of Our Country makes it easy for you to bring social studies back into your curriculum. With many features to help you reinforce what you are already teaching in reading and language arts, you can "multitask" as you teach social studies. Here's how.

Vocabulary Development

Studies have shown that vocabulary is the single strongest predictor of successful student comprehension. For this reason, key social studies terms get special treatment, identified in bold, blue type in each chapter of the Student Edition.

To help you teach these terms, the overview page for each chapter in the Lesson Guide alerts you to new vocabulary. Each Preview section in the Lesson Guide indicates when to introduce and reteach the terms. Throughout the Procedures section in the Lesson Guide, tinted sidebars at point of use suggest more ways to amplify vocabulary development. And in *Solutions for Effective Instruction,* you will find many other techniques for helping your students master new words.

High-interest Content and Reading Strategies

What better way to create lifelong readers than to introduce primary students to exciting and interesting text? Every chapter in the Student Edition of *Social Studies Alive! Regions of Our Country* has two types of reading. The first part of the chapter presents essential concepts with considerate language and pictures that students can relate to. The second part of the chapter is an engaging case study delving deeper into a chapter concept. For example, in the case study in Chapter 7, "Hurricane Andrew," students read about the hurricane and explore its impact on Florida.

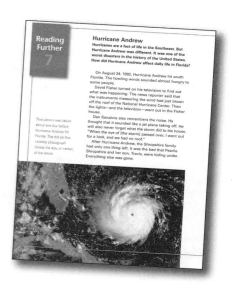

The Lesson Guide includes detailed Procedures to help you teach students how to read informational text. It also has tinted sidebars at point of use with suggestions for specific reading strategies to help students master the content.

The Interactive Student Notebook is set up to help students develop a purpose for reading, take memorable notes on what they've read, extend the concept presented in Reading Further, and synthesize what they've learned in creative ways.

Writing Assignments

Good writing is the expression of good thinking. Stating ideas clearly in writing is a key element of literacy, but it is a skill that takes constant practice to learn. Throughout the Lesson Guide, you will find careful instructions for numerous writing assignments—simple sentences, descriptions, comparisons and contrasts, stories, and personal experiences—that students will complete in their Interactive Student Notebooks in Preview, Reading Notes, Reading Further, and Processing assignments. Each chapter test also includes a prompt for student writing. As the year progresses, you will be able to see student writing progress from simple tasks to more detailed articulations.

Additional writing tips appear in tinted sidebars at point of use in the Lesson Guide and in *Solutions for Effective Instruction*.

Additional Reading Opportunities

A love of reading comes from frequent exposure to great books. To supplement *Social Studies Alive! Regions of Our Country*, each chapter in the Lesson Guide includes an annotated list of books that extend and enrich the content of the lesson. The annotated list appears on the Enhancing Learning page. Some of these books are for you to read to students, and others are books that students can read themselves.

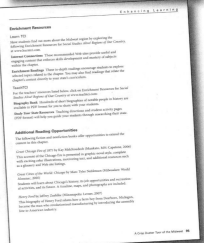

Assessing Learning

Effective assessment requires many approaches—individual and group, informal and formal—to create a well-rounded understanding of student performance. Here are some tips for evaluating student work.

Individual Participation

Assessment of day-to-day activities benefits both you and your students. You send the message that every activity is important. And by identifying what works and what doesn't, you are able to adjust your instructional plans. Try these methods:

- Make your expectations known in advance so students will know how they will be rated.
- Note a student's answers to questions, both oral and written.
- Evaluate participation in act-it-outs and class discussions.
- Look for a student's level of cooperation in a pair or small group.
- Ask students to assess their own work.
- Skim notebooks as students work in class.

Group Interaction

Evaluating groupwork presents a lot of questions: Should you rate the product or the process? The individual or the group? The amount of effort or the quality of the result? Here are five steps that will help you assess groupwork equitably:

1. Set clear criteria for evaluation.

2. Make both individuals and groups accountable.

3. Record notes as groups work and as they present their final products.

4. Have students complete self-assessments to evaluate their individual contributions as well as the group's performance.

5. Determine group and individual grades.

Formal Assessment

In addition to classroom observations and evaluation of student notebooks, you will need formal measurements of how much your students have learned. Research has shown that the TCI Approach improves student comprehension and retention. (For research results, visit www.teachtci.com.) *Social Studies Alive! Regions of Our Country* provides assessment at the end of each chapter. You will find reproducible test pages in the Lesson Masters and answers in the Lesson Guide.

Each chapter assessment has three parts. The first part, "Big Ideas," consists of multiple-choice questions. Students will find it helpful to review their Reading Notes in their Interactive Student Notebooks as preparation for these questions.

The second part, "Social Studies Skills," requires students to apply their analytical skills to maps and other visual representations of informational text, as well as to reading passages. Students reply to short-answer questions in this section. One or more questions about the Reading Further selection may appear here or in "Big Ideas."

In the third part, "Show You Know," students must use higher-order thinking skills to respond to writing prompts. These open-response questions are scaffolded to help students understand what to do.

You will find digital versions of the assessments on the TeachTCI CD-ROM, both in PDF format and in the Assessment Creator. With the Assessment Creator, you can use each test as is, randomize the order of questions, edit questions, or add your own questions.

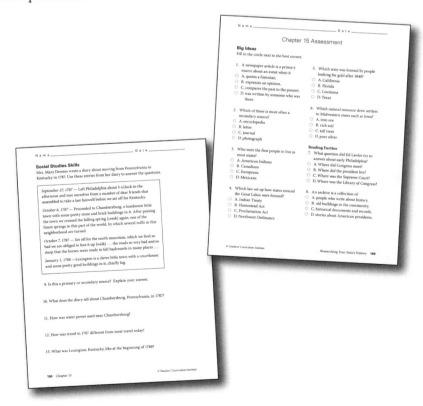

Enhancing Instruction with TeachTCI

Support for *Social Studies Alive! Regions of Our Country* extends beyond the box of print and audiovisual materials to a wealth of technology components. With the TeachTCI CD-ROM and a code that provides access to exclusive online resources, you will have the following tools to help with planning and extending the lessons and customizing your assessment.

All the Materials in the Teacher Resources Kit, in Digital Format

Access digital versions of components, such as the Lesson Guide, Lesson Masters, Interactive Student Notebook, *Sounds of Social Studies* CD, Transparencies, and Placards. All materials are organized by chapter. Preview and print items as needed.

Assessment Creator

Build customized assessments for your class. This tool lets you add, delete, edit, and sort questions and answers.

Student Edition Text

You and your students can view the Student Edition text online. You'll see what your students are reading as you assign them chapters and reading challenges.

Reading Challenges Scoring Manager

Assign reading challenges to your class and track results of both individual students and entire classes. You'll know how much your students understand and what topics need to be reinforced.

Lesson Tips from the TCI Community

Get ideas for your own classroom, engage in professional exchanges with teachers around the country, and share your own best practices. Our discussion groups are now organized by program and chapter.

Enrichment Resources

Enhance student learning with *Study Your State* Resources (student activity pages you can download) and concise, student-friendly biographies of major figures mentioned in state standards.

Customized State Correlations

See how the content you are teaching aligns to your state standards in easy-to-read chart form.

LearnTCI (Beta version available fall 2009)

LearnTCI—www.learntci.com—allows students to access their text and corresponding videos, visuals, literature, maps, and primary sources online. Students are then challenged to answer questions about what they read and experienced. LearnTCI contains:

- Student Edition text
- Text-to-Audio Tool for Accessibility
- Text Highlighting Tool
- Main Idea Viewer
- Multimedia Reading Challenges
- Classroom Discussion Groups
- Enrichment Resources

Student Edition Text

Students can read the text of their Student Edition anywhere they have access to a computer with an Internet connection.

Text-to-Audio Tool for Accessibility

Students can highlight the text and have it read to them. You can decide which students can access this feature. It is geared primarily toward English Language Learners and Students Reading Below Grade Level.

Text Highlighting Tool

Students can highlight what they think are the main ideas of each section.

Main Idea Viewer

After using the Text Highlighting Tool, students can then compare their answers to the main ideas identified by the program. Again, you can decide which students can access this feature. It is especially helpful for English Language Learners and Students Reading Below Grade Level.

Multimedia Reading Challenges

Students analyze an interactive video, visual, or primary sources related to the text and then respond to questions. In order to answer correctly, students need to read and understand the text as well as the multimedia element. Students receive immediate feedback, so if they didn't answer a question correctly, they can re-read the passage to learn the correct answer.

Classroom Discussion Groups

You and your students can have virtual class discussions on the content you are teaching. Allows peer-to-peer learning to extend beyond your class time.

Enrichment Resources

Students can now gain deeper understanding by exploring chapter-related Web sites and supplemental essays that further support state standards.

Growing Professionally

Creating long-lasting change in today's social studies classroom is hard work. You need new ideas, realistic strategies, and ongoing support.

TCI Academy, the professional development division of TCI, can help make learning come alive for all students at your school or in your district. We offer more than 20 professional development sessions for elementary teachers on topics such as content literacy, teaching American history, differentiating instruction, and many more.

TCI Academy Trainers are classroom teachers with years of experience helping their colleagues become highly successful and effective teachers. Our Trainers will partner with you to ensure your school or district receives the latest training in a highly engaging manner. In addition to on-site training, TCI Academy's on-site consulting is a powerful way for school and districts to improve instruction in social studies. On-site consulting combines direct instruction, classroom observation, and demonstration lessons to help teachers implement TCI's curricular programs and strategies to their full potential.

For a complete listing of TCI Academy sessions, please visit our Web site at www.tciacademy.com or call us at 800-840-2698.

Letter to Families

The model letter on the following page is designed to tell families what topics you will cover with *Social Studies Alive! Regions of Our Country,* how you will teach their children—using the exciting TCI Approach—and the ways you will incorporate language arts instruction into your teaching of social studies. It also includes tips on providing support at home.

Using the Letter to Families

1. *Reproduce the letter.* You may find it more effective to create your own letter based on the model provided. A customized letter might include rules and procedures that are specific to your classroom.

2. *Send the letter home with students during the first week of school.* Open the lines of communication early. The same letter, or another version of it, should also be available for Back to School Night.

3. *Encourage parents to monitor progress throughout the year by reviewing their child's Interactive Student Notebook.* The Interactive Student Notebook will give parents an overview of their child's learning. During parent conferences, you can use the Interactive Student Notebook to demonstrate where students are excelling and where they are struggling. You may want to have parents sign the Interactive Student Notebook each week to ensure that they are continually monitoring their child's progress.

Dear Families,

This year will be an exciting one for the students in my class. They will be learning key social studies concepts in a highly engaging way.

Our class is using *Social Studies Alive! Regions of Our Country,* a program that truly engages students in learning. Your child will be an active participant, experiencing social studies through innovative teaching practices that include dramatic role-playing, creative simulations, dynamic group projects, and writing activities.

Curious about what your child will be learning this year? Fourth grade is a time of giant steps in learning—not only in the three Rs, but also in learning about the regions of the United States. Some of the topics we will cover in social studies include population density and life in the Northeast, the effects of geography on life in the Southeast, agricultural changes in the Midwest, a case study in water use: the Colorado River, and cities of the West.

As the class works on social studies, I will be giving students many opportunities to practice what they are learning in reading and language arts. Your child will have an Interactive Student Notebook in which to write, draw, and answer questions. Follow your child's work in this notebook throughout the year and you will see progress not only in social studies knowledge but also in communication skills.

Here are some tips for supporting your child's academic progress in this class:

- Discuss social studies and current events with your child, and listen to what your child has to say.
- Ask to see the Interactive Student Notebook on a regular basis so you can see for yourself what your child is learning.
- Provide a quiet study place, free from distractions.
- Finally, extend learning beyond the walls of the classroom. Take your child to historical sites or museums, to local government buildings or events where you can experience civics in action, and to outdoor places or other sites that support your child's study of geography. Point out that social studies is all around us, that it shapes the present and the future and the way we live, and that every one of us can play an active and positive role in it.

Thank you in advance for your support. I am looking forward to an exciting, enjoyable, and enriching year working with you and your child.

Sincerely,

Your child's teacher

Discovering the Social Sciences

What do social scientists do?

Overview

Students learn why the study of the social sciences is important to understanding human behavior. In the Preview activity, they explore why studying familiar subjects is important. Each student brings four personal artifacts to class, such as an old family photograph or an advertisement for a toy they would like to purchase. In a Response Group activity, students discuss the artifacts from the perspective of each of these social science traditions: economics, geography, political science, and history. They learn that the social sciences offer powerful ways to understand individuals and society. In Reading Further, students explore how archaeologists use artifacts to understand the past. In the Processing activity, students complete a project specific to a social scientist of their choosing.

Objectives

Social Studies
- Create simple definitions for the terms *economist, geographer, political scientist*, and *historian*.
- Identify artifacts that social scientists use in their research.
- Draw conclusions from examination of artifacts from an archaeological perspective.

Language Arts
- Present and support choices. (speaking)

Social Studies Vocabulary

social scientist, social science, economist, economy, geographer, political scientist, historian, archaeologist

Materials

Social Studies Alive! Regions of Our Country

Transparency 1

Interactive Student Notebooks

Lesson Masters
- Student Handouts 1A and 1B
- Information Master 1

paper bags

newspaper

trash from class trash can

Time Estimates

Preview: 20 min.

Response Group Activity: 2 sessions (45 min. each)

Reading Further: 30 min.

Processing: 30 min.

Activity	Suggested Time	Materials
Preview • Connecting to Prior Knowledge • Developing Vocabulary • Building Background Knowledge	20 minutes	• *Social Studies Alive! Regions of Our Country*, Section 1.1 • Interactive Student Notebooks
Response Group Activity Examining artifacts from the perspective of four different social scientists	*Phase 1* 45 minutes • Defining the different social scientists (Steps 1–5) *Phase 2* 45 minutes • Examining artifacts (Steps 6–9)	• *Social Studies Alive! Regions of Our Country*, Sections 1.2–1.6 and Summary • Interactive Student Notebooks • Student Handouts 1A and 1B (1 copy of each per student) • Information Master 1 (1 transparency) • paper bags (for groups' artifacts)
Reading Further Exploring Cahokia as an archaeologist	30 minutes	• *Social Studies Alive! Regions of Our Country*, Chapter 1 Reading Further • Transparency 1 • Interactive Student Notebooks • newspaper • trash from class trash can
Processing Thinking like a social scientist	30 minutes	• Interactive Student Notebooks
Assessment	30 minutes	• Chapter 1 Assessment, Lesson Masters • Chapter 1 Assessment, Digital Teacher Resources

Preview

1 **Connecting to Prior Knowledge:** Introduce the study of the social sciences by connecting to students' study of other subjects.

- Introduce the Interactive Student Notebook. Then have students complete Preview 1 to identify the importance of certain subjects they study in school.

- Afterward, tell students that they will be learning about the social sciences with you. Tell students that the social sciences are concerned with people's behavior and the explanations for that behavior. Explain that students will learn to think like social scientists throughout the year and that this is the first lesson in their training as social scientists. As the year progresses, they will put on various social scientist "hats" to develop different ways of thinking about human behavior.

2 **Developing Vocabulary:** Introduce key social studies terms—*social scientist, social science, economist, economy, geographer, political scientist, historian,* and *archaeologist.*

- Discuss each term before beginning the activity, using methods described in *Solutions for Effective Instruction.*

- Review each term again with students as it appears in the activity reading, and encourage them to use it in their writing.

3 **Building Background Knowledge:** Introduce and discuss four types of social scientists.

- Have students read Section 1.1 in *Social Studies Alive! Regions of Our Country.*

- Draw students' attention to the graphic organizer in Section 1.1. Lead a class discussion by asking: *Who are the people pictured here? What are they wearing? From the symbols on their hats, what might you guess an economist would be interested in? A geographer? A political scientist? A historian? What might be interesting about these fields of study? How might these fields of study help us better understand people?*

> **Vocabulary Development: Match Words and Definitions**
>
> Have each student create a set of social studies vocabulary cards. Have students write each key social studies term on one card and its definition on another card. Then ask students to spread out the cards and match the words with their definitions.

Response Groups

Phase 1: Learning About Social Scientists

1 **Introduce the activity.** Assign students to mixed-ability pairs and tell them that in this activity, they will use information from the Student Edition to learn what social scientists study and discover. Have students turn to Reading Notes 1 in their Interactive Student Notebooks. Explain that they will use what they learn from the Student Edition to decorate hats that represent an economist, a geographer, a political scientist, and a historian.

2 **Have students read Section 1.2 in the Student Edition.** As they finish, have them complete the related section of the Reading Notes by decorating the hat for the appropriate social scientist.

3 **As a class, create a simple definition of the term** *economist.* Lead a class discussion by asking students to share the words and symbols they used on their economist hat. Clarify any questions they have. Then create a simple definition of the term *economist.* Write it on the board or on a large sheet of paper.

4 **Repeat Steps 2 and 3 for Sections 1.3 through 1.5, and create simple definitions for the other three types of social scientists.**

5 **Have students read Sections 1.6 and the Summary.** Review the information about artifacts with them.

Phase 2: Thinking like Social Scientists

6 **Several days in advance of Phase 2, distribute a copy of** *Student Handout 1A: Collecting Social Science Artifacts* **to each student.** Encourage students to begin gathering artifacts and completing the corresponding written assignment right away. (**Note:** The directions for artifact collection call for small objects, but the size of the artifacts that students bring to class is completely up to you. You may want to allow students to collect larger artifacts and place them in a box or large shopping bag.) The handout provides some examples of appropriate artifacts; here are some more:

- economics artifact: a product from the kitchen

- geography artifact: a picture of a family trip

- political science artifact: a political cartoon

- history artifact: an old letter or postcard

7 **Prepare for the activity.** Make enough copies of *Student Handout 1B: Analyzing Artifacts* to give one copy to each student. Assign students to mixed-ability groups of four. If necessary, prepare a transparency that shows students where to sit and who their group members are. Be sure students have their artifacts when they assemble their groups.

8 **Introduce the activity.** Tell students that in their groups, they will be discussing the artifacts they have brought from home.

9 **Conduct the activity.** Project a transparency of *Information Master 1: Sharing and Discussing Artifacts.* Walk students through the activity, covering the text on the transparency with a sheet of paper that you move down to reveal and read aloud each step.

- At Step 5, hand out one copy of Student Handout 1B to each student. Students will use the handouts to identify artifacts that social scientists use in their research and to record their conclusions about each artifact.

Reading Strategy: Make and Check Predictions

Before partners read, have them glance at the title of each section and list all the words related to the topic they think will appear in that section. As they read, tell them to watch to see if their predictions are correct. After they finish reading, have them review their original list and put a check mark by words that did appear in each section. Then discuss why the other words might not have been there.

Student Handouts 1A and 1B

Information Master 1

- For Step 6, make clear to students that economists, geographers, political scientists, and historians often study similar artifacts. For example, a historian might be interested in an old postcard because it is an artifact from the past. An economist might be interested in the same artifact because the postcard was purchased, which reveals something about the economic choices people made. A geographer might be interested in the postcard because it reveals where people traveled. Encourage debate, but help students understand that there are many correct answers.

Reading Further: Clues from Cahokia

Transparency 1

1 **Project** *Transparency 1: Monks Mound at Cahokia.* Ask the following visual discovery questions to help students analyze the image carefully and make some predictions:

- What do you see in this photograph?

- Do you think the mound is a natural feature or a human feature?

- Who do you think built it?

- When do you think people might have built the mound?

- Why might people have built the mound? What do you think its purpose was?

- How might a social scientist begin to prove his or her guesses? What clues would you hope to find?

2 **Explain that this is a picture of Monks Mound in southern Illinois.** Tell students that Monks Mound is the largest of 70 mounds in southern Illinois. When social scientists examined the mounds, they discovered that they were part of a 1300-year-old American Indian city called Cahokia. Explain that students are going to read about Cahokia and find out how social scientists used discoveries made there to learn about the past.

3 **Have students read, independently or in small groups, Reading Further 1 in the Student Edition.**

4 **To help students understand how social scientists draw conclusions from observations, have them undertake the process themselves.**

- Tell students they are going to work as archaeologists to examine artifacts from our own culture.

- Spread a newspaper on the ground and carefully empty the contents of your class trash can onto the newspaper. Spread out the trash so that each object can be seen (you might want to use a pencil rather than your hands).

- Ask students to open their Interactive Student Notebooks to Reading Further 1. Have them read the directions and complete the activity.

- If time permits, have students share their conclusions with the class.

Processing

1 **Have students apply what they have learned to complete Processing 1 in their Interactive Student Notebooks.** Have them use one of the Extra Student Work pages at the back of the Interactive Student Notebook.

2 **If time permits, have students share with the class their responses to the Processing activity.**

Assessment

Masters for the chapter assessment appear in the *Lesson Masters*. Answers appear below.

Big Ideas

1. B		6. D	
2. A		7. C	
3. B		8. A	
4. B		9. D	
5. C			

Social Studies Skills

10. An economist would be most interested in talking to the children because they are selling a service to meet people's wants or needs. (Wording may vary.)

11. computer, table, shirt, paper (Accept any item in the picture except the boys, trees, or grass.)

12. The trees are natural features because trees grow in nature; they are not made by people. (Wording may vary.)

13. Answers may vary. Possible answers: Where does this scene take place? Where did the computers come from?

14. Answers may vary. Possible answer: so that people in the future can know what life was like today.

Show You Know

15. The bulleted points in the instructions can serve as a rubric for this item.

English Language Learners

Have students work with a partner during the last step of the Response Group activity, when groups share their conclusions about their artifacts. Students can write down their conclusions and have their partner read them, or they can dictate their conclusions to their partner and then read the written statement aloud to the class.

Students with Special Needs

Collect four different kinds of hats (possibly from a secondhand store) and allow students to attach artifacts appropriate to one social scientist to each of them. This will give students a visual to refer to throughout this lesson. This will also give students the opportunity to actually put on the hat of a social scientist, which may motivate students during the Processing activity.

Enrichment

Have students gather information about the community in which they live. Tell them to then categorize their information into four groups—economics, geography, political science, and history. Students may then put together a presentation about their community from the point of view of each of the social scientists. This may be a good presentation to share with other classes or grade levels.

Enrichment Resources

LearnTCI

Have students find out more about economics and researching the economy of their state by exploring the following Enrichment Resources for *Social Studies Alive! Regions of Our Country,* at www.learntci.com.

Internet Connections These recommended Web sites provide useful and engaging content that enforces skills development and mastery of subjects within the chapter.

Enrichment Readings These in-depth readings encourage students to explore selected topics related to the chapter. You may also find readings that relate the chapter's content directly to your state's curriculum.

TeachTCI

For the teachers' resources listed below, click on Enrichment Resources for *Social Studies Alive! Regions of Our Country* at www.teachtci.com.

Biography Bank Hundreds of short biographies of notable people in history are available in PDF format for you to share with your students.

***Study Your State* Resources** Teaching directions and student activity pages (PDF format) will help you guide your students through researching their state.

Additional Reading Opportunities

The following fiction and nonfiction books offer opportunities to extend the content in this chapter.

Archaeology for Kids: Uncovering the Mysteries of Our Past by Richard Panchyk (Chicago: Chicago Review Press, 2001)

This interactive book combines information about archaeology and archaeological methods. In addition to chapters on the first civilizations, historical maps, cave art, and carbon dating, 25 activities are included to help students understand how archaeologists make discoveries.

Hottest, Coldest, Highest, Deepest by Steve Jenkins (New York: Houghton Mifflin, 1998)

This geography resource explores amazing places on Earth. Information about the highest mountain, the longest river, the deepest lake, and other extremes is presented with collage-style illustrations and helpful graphs and charts.

House, House by Jane Yolen (New York: Marshall Cavendish, 1998)

From 1882 to 1907, the Howes family took more than 20,000 photographs of buildings and people in small towns and villages throughout New England. In the 1990s, photographer Jason Stemple traveled to Hatfield, Massachusetts, and took photographs of some of the same houses. This "then and now" book features pairings of old and new photographs. The text adds interesting facts about the past and present.

The House on Maple Street by Bonnie Pryor (New York: Mulberry, 1987)

While digging in their garden, a family finds an arrowhead and a tiny china teacup. This story traces the 300-year history of a piece of land, from the days of the buffalo to the present, to give students a sense of history through the generations.

Money, Money, Money by Eve Drobot (Toronto: Maple Tree, 2004)

This book introduces students to the history of money and trade. Interesting information about the origins of various names for currency, the minting of money, and simple economics is also included.

Exploring Regions of the United States

How do geographers study the regions of the United States?

Overview

Students apply basic map skills to learn about the regions of the United States. In the Preview activity, they draw a map of their own home showing its different "regions." In a Social Studies Skill Builder, they interpret a series of special-purpose maps depicting five regions of the United States and attempt to identify the locations at which five images of the United States were taken. In Reading Further, students discover why the Mississippi River is the most important river in the United States. In the Processing activity, students use their new map skills to explore three locations of their choice.

Objectives

Social Studies

- Interpret a physical map of the United States by using directions and latitude and longitude.
- Interpret special-purpose maps: elevation, annual rainfall, and population density.
- Hypothesize the locations of five photographs, using geographic information.
- Analyze the relationship between river systems and people.
- Research geographic information.

Language Arts

- Write reasons to support answers. (writing)

Social Studies Vocabulary

scale, map key, line of latitude, line of longitude, global grid, special-purpose map, coastal plain, inland, plateau, basin, levee

Materials

Social Studies Alive! Regions of Our Country

Transparencies 2A–2I

Interactive Student Notebooks

Lesson Masters:

- Student Handouts 2A and 2B
- Information Master 2

Interactive Desk Maps

coins

classroom map of the United States

Time Estimates

Preview: 40 min.

Social Studies Skill Builder: 3 sessions (45 min. each)

Reading Further: 30 min.

Processing: 45 min.

Activity	Suggested Time	Materials
Preview • Connecting to Prior Knowledge • Building Background Knowledge • Developing Vocabulary	40 minutes	• *Social Studies Alive! Regions of Our Country*, Section 2.1 • Interactive Student Notebooks
Social Studies Skill Builder Learning basic map skills, interpreting special-purpose maps, and identifying regions of the United States	*Phase 1* 45-minute session • Learning basic map skills (Steps 1–5)	• *Social Studies Alive! Regions of Our Country*, Sections 2.2–2.6 • Transparency 2A • Interactive Student Notebooks • Student Handout 2A (depending on class size, 1 or 2 copies, cut apart) • Interactive Desk Maps (1 per pair) • coins (1 per pair)
	Phase 2 45-minute session • Interpreting special-purpose maps (Steps 6–11)	• *Social Studies Alive! Regions of Our Country*, Section 2.7 • Transparencies 2B–2D • Interactive Student Notebooks • Student Handout 2B (depending on class size, 1 or 2 copies, cut apart) • Interactive Desk Maps (1 per pair) • coins (1 per pair)
	Phase 3 45-minute session • Identifying regions (Steps 12–14)	• *Social Studies Alive! Regions of Our Country*, Sections 2.8–2.10, Summary • Transparencies 2E–2I • Interactive Student Notebooks • Interactive Desk Maps (1 per pair)
Reading Further Exploring the Mississippi River	30 minutes	• *Social Studies Alive! Regions of Our Country*, Chapter 2 Reading Further • Interactive Student Notebooks • Information Master 2 • classroom map of the United States
Processing Using new map skills to acquire information about locations	45 minutes	• *Social Studies Alive! Regions of Our Country*, Chapter 2 • Interactive Student Notebooks • Interactive Desk Maps
Assessment	30 minutes	• Chapter 2 Assessment, Lesson Masters • Chapter 2 Assessment, Digital Teacher Resources

Preview

1 **Connecting to Prior Knowledge:** Introduce maps and regions by asking students to draw a map of their home.

- Have students open their Interactive Student Notebooks to Preview 2 and draw a picture of their home from a bird's-eye view. Tell them to label each room (bedroom, kitchen, living room, and so on) and the other main parts of their home (hallway, porch, stairs, and so on).

- Once they have drawn a map of their home, have them choose a color for each of five "regions" of their home. All bedrooms, for example, might be blue; all outdoor porches might be red. Finally, have students create a simple key with the names of each of the five regions of their homes.

- When they have finished, have them share their drawings with others in the class and explain how and why they created their five regions. Ask students to explain what sets each region of their home apart from the others.

2 **Building Background Knowledge:** Introduce the five themes of geography and establish the last theme—regions—as a primary focus of students' social studies work this year.

- Introduce Chapter 2 of *Social Studies Alive! Regions of Our Country.* Tell students that in this chapter, they will practice basic map skills as they learn about the five regions of the United States. Have students read Section 2.1.

- Conduct a brief review of the five themes of geography by asking volunteers to share their answers to the questions in Section 2.1 as they apply to their school. Let them know that throughout the year they will be exploring different regions of the United States.

- Introduce the graphic organizer in Section 2.1. Ask students to examine the graphic organizer. Then ask: *What five regions are labeled on the map of the United States? In which region of the United States is our school?*

3 **Developing Vocabulary:** Introduce key social studies terms—*scale, map key, line of latitude, line of longitude, global grid, special-purpose map, coastal plain, inland, plateau, basin,* and *levee.*

- Discuss each term before beginning the activity, using methods described in *Solutions for Effective Instruction.*

- Review each term again with students as it appears in the activity reading, and encourage them to use it in their writing.

> **Vocabulary Development: Define Words**
>
> Have the class make a picture dictionary. On a large sheet of paper, create a class list of the social studies terms covered in the lesson. For each word, have a volunteer come up to the paper and create an illustration that represents its meaning.

Social Studies Skill Builder

Phase 1: Learning Basic Map Skills

1   **Prepare for the first Geography Challenge.** Make enough copies of *Student Handout 2A: Geography Challenge 2A Cards* to give each pair one Geography Challenge card and have a few extras. (It is helpful to have a pool for students to pick from, in case other pairs are still using their cards.) Then cut out the cards. (**Note:** You may want to laminate the cards for future use.) Assign students to pairs and seat them side by side at desks facing the front of the classroom. Give each pair an Interactive Desk Map and a coin.

Student Handout 2A

2   **Introduce the activity.** Explain to students that they will practice basic map skills as they learn about five regions of the United States: the Northeast, Southeast, Midwest, Southwest, and West. Tell students that when they have completed three Geography Challenges, they will have the skills and knowledge they need to begin a deeper exploration of each of our nation's five regions.

3   **Have students read Sections 2.2 through 2.6 in their Student Editions.** Tell them that they will use all the skills they read about during the first Geography Challenge.

4   **Practice basic map skills with students.** Project *Transparency 2A: The United States.* Ask pairs to take out a pencil and turn their Interactive Desk Maps to the side showing the single large map of the United States. (**Note:** You may want to tell students that this is a physical and political map of the United States. Also, you may need to show students how to trace the path of the longitude and latitude lines over land areas.) Give students the following tasks, allowing time for them to complete each task. Use Transparency 2A to model each answer:

Interactive Desk Map

a.   Place your coin on the compass rose. What are the four main directions? (*north, east, south, west*)

b.   What do we call the four main directions? (*cardinal directions*)

c.   Place your pencil pointing north on the map. (*Pencils should point north.*)

d.   Place your pencil pointing east on the map. (*Pencils should point east.*)

e.   Place your pencil pointing southwest on the map. (*Pencils should point southwest.*)

f.   What do we call directions such as southwest? (*intermediate directions*)

g.   Place your pencil pointing northeast on the map. (*Pencils should point northeast.*)

Transparency 2A

h.   Lay your pencil along 35 degrees north latitude. (*Pencils should be placed on the 35th parallel of north latitude.*)

i.   Lay your pencil along 45 degrees north latitude. (*Pencils should be placed on the 45th parallel of north latitude.*)

j. Lay your pencil along 90 degrees west longitude. (*Pencils should be placed on the 90th meridian of west longitude.*)

k. Lay your pencil along 115 degrees west longitude. (*Pencils should be placed on the 115th meridian of west longitude.*)

l. Place your coin on 45 degrees north latitude, 80 degrees west longitude. Which country are you in? (*Canada*)

m. Place your coin on 40 degrees north latitude, 115 degrees west longitude. Which state are you in? (*Nevada*)

5 Have students take Geography Challenge 2A to test their new knowledge of maps.

- Pass out a Geography Challenge 2A card to each pair.

- Have students open their Interactive Student Notebooks to Geography Challenge 2A. Let them know that they will write the answers to each challenge card on this page.

- Tell students to use their Interactive Desk Maps during this activity.

- As pairs finish each challenge card, use Guide to Geography Challenge 2A to correct their work. Award pairs one point for a correct answer. If their answer is incorrect, give them the option of trying a second time. After scoring, lay the cards out on the table in front of you and allow students to choose their next Geography Challenge 2A question.

- Continue until pairs have answered all the questions.

Phase 2: Interpreting Special-Purpose Maps

6 Prepare for the second Geography Challenge. Make enough copies of *Student Handout 2B: Geography Challenge 2B Cards* to give each pair one Geography Challenge card and have a few extras. Then cut out the cards. Assign students to pairs and seat them side by side at desks facing the front of the classroom. Give each pair an Interactive Desk Map and a coin.

7 Have students read Section 2.7 in their Student Edition. Explain that during the second Geography Challenge they will be using the skills they read about here.

8 Practice reading an elevation map with students. Project *Transparency 2B: Elevation Map of the United States.* Ask pairs to locate the elevation map of the United States on their Interactive Desk Maps. Give pairs the following tasks, allowing time for them to accomplish each task. Use Transparency 2B to model each answer:

a. Place your coin anywhere on the map at sea level. (*Coins should be placed on ocean areas of the map.*)

b. Place your coin anywhere on the map that is between 0 and 1,000 feet in elevation. (*Coins should be placed on light green areas.*)

c. Place your coin anywhere on the map that is between 1,000 and 5,000 feet in elevation. (*Coins should be placed on yellow areas.*)

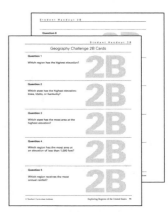

Student Handout 2B

Transparency 2B

d. Place your coin anywhere on the map that is between 5,000 and 10,000 feet in elevation. (*Coins should be placed on orange areas.*)

e. Place your coin anywhere that is above 10,000 feet in elevation. (*Coins should be placed on brown areas.*)

9 Practice reading an annual rainfall map with students. Project *Transparency 2C: Annual Rainfall Map of the United States.* Ask students to find the annual rainfall map of the United States on their Interactive Desk Maps. Give pairs the following tasks, allowing time for them to accomplish each task. Use Transparency 2C to model each answer:

a. Place your coin anywhere on the map that receives fewer than 16 inches of rain per year. (*Coins should be placed on orange areas of the map.*)

b. Place your coin anywhere on the map that receives more than 96 inches of rain per year. (*Coins should be placed on dark green areas.*)

c. Place your coin anywhere on the map that receives between 32 and 64 inches of rain per year. (*Coins should be placed on light green areas.*)

Transparency 2C

10 Practice reading a population density map with students. Project *Transparency 2D: Population Density Map of the United States.* Ask students to locate the population density map of the United States on their Interactive Desk Maps. Give pairs the following tasks, allowing time for them to accomplish each task. Use Transparency 2D to model each answer:

a. Place your coin anywhere on the map where less than 10 people per square mile live. (*Coins should be placed on light yellow areas of the map.*)

b. Place your coin anywhere on the map where more than 250 people per square mile live. (*Coins should be placed on purple areas.*)

c. Place your coin anywhere on the map where between 50 and 250 people per square mile live. (*Coins should be placed on dark orange areas.*)

Transparency 2D

11 Have students take Geography Challenge 2B to test their new knowledge of special-purpose maps.

• Pass out a Geography Challenge 2B card to each pair.

• Have students open their Interactive Student Notebooks to Geography Challenge 2B. Let them know that they will write the answers to each challenge card on this page.

• Tell students to use their Interactive Desk Maps during this activity.

• As pairs finish each challenge card, use Guide to Geography Challenge 2B to correct their work. Award pairs one point for a correct answer. If their answer is incorrect, give them the option of trying a second time. After scoring, lay the cards out on the table in front of you and allow students to choose their next Geography Challenge 2B question.

• Continue until pairs have answered all the questions.

Phase 3: Identifying Regions of the United States

12 Prepare for the third Geography Challenge. Assign students to pairs and seat them side by side at desks facing the front of the classroom. Give each pair an Interactive Desk Map.

13 Have students read Sections 2.8 through 2.10 and the Summary in their Student Editions. Tell them they will be using the information they read about the five regions of the United States—the Northeast, Southeast, Midwest, Southwest, and West—during the third Geography Challenge.

14 Have students take Geography Challenge 2C to test their ability to identify regions of the United States.

- Tell students they will use their new map skills and knowledge of regions of the United States to identify where each of five photographs of communities and physical landmarks were taken. They should use their Student Editions and Interactive Desk Maps as resources as they try to determine the exact location of each image.

- Project *Transparency 2E: Where Are We?* Cover the clues with a sheet of paper. As students try to determine where the image was taken, slide the paper down to expose one clue at a time, hiding the answer at the bottom. Uncover as many clues as students need to venture a reasonable guess about the photograph's location. Ask students not to shout out their answers. Direct them to write their answers on Geography Challenge 2C in their Interactive Student Notebooks. When all pairs are ready, reveal the answer.

- Repeat the procedure for *Transparencies 2F–2I: Where Are We?*

Transparencies 2E–2I

Reading Further: The Mighty Mississippi

1 Read students a passage from Mark Twain's *The Adventures of Huckleberry Finn.*

- Tell students that you are going to read them a passage from a story, but do not tell them the name of the story or that it takes place on a river.

- Ask them to listen carefully and try to picture themselves in the scene. Have them pay special attention to what they see, hear, smell, and feel, and have them use these clues to help them figure out where they are. You can suggest that they close their eyes while they listen to help them picture themselves in this place.

- You may want to tell students that there will be some unfamiliar words in the passage. Let them know they should still be able to figure out where they are.

- Read *Information Master 2: On the River* aloud to students.

Information Master 2

2 After reading, ask the following questions to help students analyze the passage and make some predictions:

- Where were you?

- What sights did you see? What sounds did you hear? What did you feel? Smell? (Give students some time to describe details they remember.)

- Which details helped you figure out where you were?

- Is this a place you would want to visit? Why or why not?

- Is this a real place? Why do you think that? (After students have had a chance to guess, you can let them know that, even though this is a fictional story, it is set on a real river. Tell them that the river is the largest river in the United States, but don't tell them the name yet.)

3 Using a classroom map of the United States, have students make and defend guesses about which river they just visited. Ask them to point to their guess on the map and explain their choice.

4 After students finish making predictions, introduce the Mississippi River.

- Let students know that the passage they just heard comes from a book called *The Adventures of Huckleberry Finn* by Mark Twain. In the story, a boy named Huck and a slave named Jim are are on a raft on the Mississippi River—the largestand most used river in the United States.

- If students have not already found the Mississippi River on the classroom map, point it out. Tell them they are about to read all about the Mississippi River.

5 Have students read, independently or in small groups, Reading Further 2 in the Student Edition.

6 To help students understand how large an area of the United States is affected by the Mississippi River, have students use a map to ask and answer questions about the Mississippi River basin.

- Ask students to open their Interactive Student Notebooks to Reading Further 2. Have them read the directions and complete the "Questions" portion of the page.

- Have pairs take turns asking each other questions about the Mississippi, completing the "Answers" portion of the page as they work. (**Option:** If time permits, you could instead divide the class into two teams and have them ask and answer questions in a quiz show format.)

Processing

1 Have students complete Processing 2 in their Interactive Student Notebooks. Students will need to consult their Interactive Desk Maps and Student Editions to complete the assignment.

> ### Speaking and Listening: Retell a Story Aloud
>
> After reading the passage to students, ask a few volunteers to retell the story aloud. Students may have trouble recalling the full passage. Encouage them to take one minute to record the details they do remember in the correct order before telling them aloud. Then read the passage aloud again, having students listen carefully for the details they missed.

Assessment

Masters for the chapter assessment appear in the *Lesson Masters*.
Answers appear below.

Big Ideas

1. D
2. C
3. D
4. A

5. B
6. A
7. C
8. B

Social Studies Skills

9. B
10. A
11. Midwest
12. Midwest, Southeast
13. Southwest, Southeast
14. West

Show You Know

15. The bulleted points in the instructions can serve as a rubric for this item.

English Language Learners

Give students more time to work on vocabulary and become familiar with the new language introduced in this lesson. Consider having students keep a vocabulary journal to record the new terms throughout the year. During activities, put students into mixed-ability pairs so they have a partner from whom they can learn. Allow students to use completed Reading Notes and Geography Challenge pages, as well as vocabulary resources, on any assessments.

Students with Special Needs

Give students extra time to work on vocabulary and become familiar with the new language introduced in the lesson. Provide them with a printed copy of the vocabulary and definitions. Allow them to use this as a resource throughout the lesson. During the Reading Further activity, read the feature aloud to students and explain any new vocabulary.

Enrichment

Have students think of various places that they would like to visit across the country. Have them write to both the visitors bureau of each state and the chamber of commerce for each city and ask for information. When they get a response, have them locate the place on a classroom map of the United States, using a sticky note or thumb tack. Display the information and materials they receive when the class studies the appropriate region.

Enrichment Resources

LearnTCI

Have students find out more about map skills and regions of the United States by exploring the following Enrichment Resources for *Social Studies Alive! Regions of Our Country,* at www.learntci.com.

Internet Connections These recommended Web sites provide useful and engaging content that enforces skills development and mastery of subjects within the chapter.

Enrichment Readings These in-depth readings encourage students to explore selected topics related to the chapter. You may also find readings that relate the chapter's content directly to your state's curriculum.

TeachTCI

For the teachers' resources listed below, click on Enrichment Resources for *Social Studies Alive! Regions of Our Country* at www.teachtci.com:

Biography Bank Hundreds of short biographies of notable people in history are available in PDF format for you to share with your students.

***Study Your State* Resources** Teaching directions and student activity pages (PDF format) will help you guide your students through researching their state.

Additional Reading Opportunities

The following fiction and nonfiction books offer opportunities to extend the content in this chapter.

Geography from A to Z: A Picture Glossary by Jack Knowlton (New York: HarperCollins, 1988)

This book is a classic resource, with illustrations and definitions of just about every geographical term students will need to know.

Maps and Plans by Pam Robson (Brookfield, CN: Stargazer, 2005)
This book provides detailed information about various types of maps. It also includes mapping projects about direction, coordinates, fixing position, and projection. A glossary and index are included.

National Geographic Our Fifty States by Mark H. Bockenhauer and Stephen F. Cunha (Washington, D.C.: National Geographic Children's Books, 2004)

This reference features a brief history of each state, along with maps, photographs, and information. Students can use it to practice locating states, cities, and physical features.

Purple Mountain Majesties by Barbara Younger. Illustrations by Stacey Schuett. (New York: Puffin, 2002)

This story traces the journey across the United States that inspired the song "America the Beautiful." Beautiful illustrations of Niagara Falls, Chicago, and "amber waves of grain" take the reader on a historical trip across the country.

Stringbean's Trip to the Shining Sea by Vera B. and Jennifer Williams (New York: HarperTrophy, 1999)

Stringbean Coe and his brother take a trip across the United States and send a series of postcards to their family. There are postcards from several locations in the United States. The page following each postcard includes a message with information about that place.

Follow the directions on the Geography Challenge cards.
Use your Interactive Desk Map to help you.

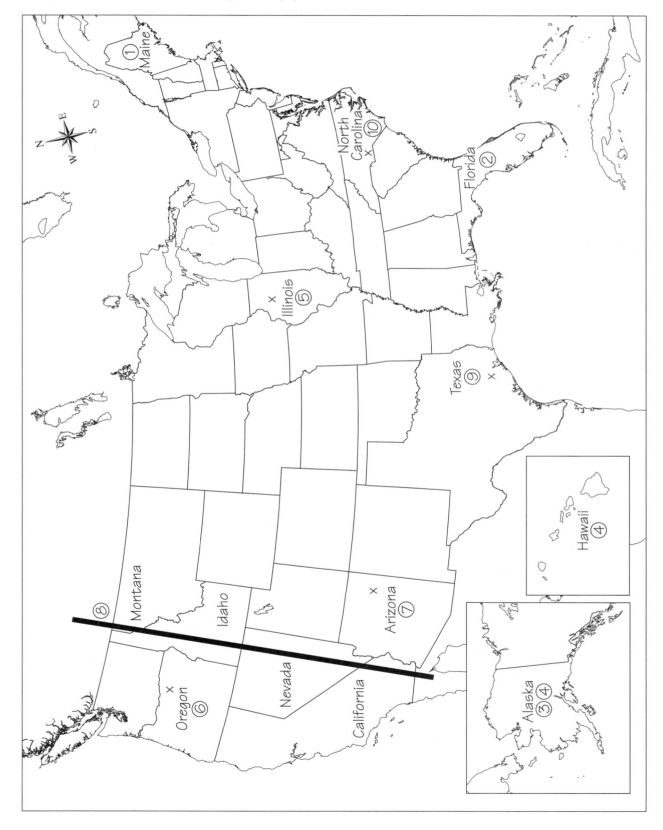

Answer each Geography Challenge 2B card in the correct space below.

Question 1   Which region has the highest elevation?
West

Question 2   Which state has the highest elevation: Iowa, Idaho, or Kentucky?
Idaho

Question 3   Which state has the most area at the highest elevation?
Colorado

Question 4   Which region has the most area at an elevation of less than 1,000 feet?
Southeast

Question 5   Which region receives the most annual rainfall?
Southeast

Question 6   Which region receives the least annual rainfall?
West

Question 7   Which state receives the least annual rainfall?
Nevada

Question 8   Which region has the highest population density
(most people per square mile)?
Northeast

Question 9   Which two regions have the lowest population densities
(fewest people per square mile)?
West, Southwest

Question 10   Which three states have the lowest population densities
(fewest people per square mile)?
Accept any three of the following: Wyoming, Alaska, North Dakota,
Montana, South Dakota.

The Peopling of the United States

How have different groups contributed to the United States?

Overview

Students learn how five ethnic groups—American Indians, Latinos, European Americans, African Americans, and Asian Americans—came to this country and contributed to its growth and development. In the Preview activity, students think about some contributions that are already a part of their lives. In a Social Studies Skill Builder, students work in pairs to read about one of the groups and draw images and symbols to represent that group's experience. Then students create a class collage that depicts American diversity. In Reading Further, students learn about layers of history in New York City and discover how people from the past have helped shape the present. During the Processing activity, they write a verse to a song that relates to each of the groups they have learned about.

Objectives

Social Studies

- Transfer information from the text to drawings about the settlement stories of ethnic groups.
- Identify key contributions to American society made by the five ethnic groups.
- Identify where the people who first settled in students' neighborhoods or towns came from.

Language Arts

- Write lyrics to a song that celebrates American diversity. (writing)

Social Studies Vocabulary

culture, diverse, the Americas, American Indian, colony, Latino, immigrant, European American, democracy, African American, Asian American, tenement

Materials

Social Studies Alive! Regions of Our Country

Transparencies 3A–3C

Interactive Student Notebooks

Lesson Masters

- Student Handout 3
- Information Master 3

drawing paper, assorted sizes

butcher paper

research materials

Time Estimates

Preview: 30 min.

Social Studies Skill Builder: 60 min.

Reading Further: 30 min.

Processing: 30 min.

Activity	Suggested Time	Materials
Preview • Connecting to Prior Knowledge • Building Background Knowledge • Developing Vocabulary	30 minutes	• *Social Studies Alive! Regions of Our Country*, Section 3.1 • Interactive Student Notebooks
Social Studies Skill Builder Creating a collage that showcases the diversity of people in the United States	60 minutes • Learning about groups and creating a collage (Steps 1–10)	• *Social Studies Alive! Regions of Our Country*, Sections 3.2–3.11 and Summary • Transparency 3A • Interactive Student Notebooks • Student Handout 3 (1 copy per pair) • Information Master 3 (1 transparency) • drawing paper (assorted sizes, 5–10 per pair) • butcher paper (1 large sheet)
Reading Further Exploring layers of history in New York City	30 minutes	• *Social Studies Alive! Regions of Our Country,* Chapter 3 Reading Further • Transparencies 3B and 3C • Interactive Student Notebooks • research materials
Processing Writing song lyrics	30 minutes	• Interactive Student Notebooks
Assessment	30 minutes	• Chapter 3 Assessment, Lesson Masters • Chapter 3 Assessment, Digital Teacher Resources

Preview

1 **Connecting to Prior Knowledge:** Introduce the idea that many different groups of people have made contributions to the United States by asking students to think about some things that are already a part of their lives.

- Have students complete Preview 3 in their Interactive Student Notebooks and share their responses about what they would miss the most if certain things were no longer part of their lives.

- Afterward, tell students that for centuries, people from all over the world have come to North America. Explain that each ethnic group has made contributions to American society. Some of these contributions are on the list they have just discussed. Without any one group and its contributions, the United States would not be the same as it is today.

2 **Building Background Knowledge:** Introduce the United States as one of the most diverse nations in the world.

- Tell students that they will learn about people from five parts of the world who have helped make the United States so interesting. Students will learn how each of these groups settled in North America and then will examine some contributions each group has made to American society.

- Have students read Section 3.1 in *Social Studies Alive! Regions of Our Country*.

- Introduce the graphic organizer in Section 3.1, and ask these questions: *What do you see? How does each thing pictured make the United States a varied country? How would our lives be different if one or all of these things were not a part of our society?*

3 **Developing Vocabulary:** Introduce key social studies terms—*culture, diverse, the Americas, American Indian, colony, Latino, immigrant, European American, democracy, African American, Asian American,* and *tenement*.

- Discuss each term before beginning the activity, using methods described in *Solutions for Effective Instruction*.

- Review each term again with students as it appears in the activity reading, and encourage them to use it in their writing.

Social Studies Skill Builder

1 **Prepare for the activity.** Before class, make enough copies of *Student Handout 3: Creating a Class Collage* to give one to each pair. In class, assign students to mixed-ability pairs.

2 **Introduce the activity.** Tell students that they will work as a class to create a collage that tells how different groups of people settled in the United States and what each group's contributions were. Explain that students will work in pairs to draw images or symbols that represent the group assigned to them.

Student Handout 3

3 **Introduce the elements of a collage.** Project *Transparency 3A: Contributions to the United States.* Ask students: *What do you see? How is a collage different from other kinds of illustrations? Why might artists use collages to express themselves?* Tell students to keep the following things in mind as they prepare to create and assemble their collage:

Transparency 3A

- Collages are made by combining different images and graphic elements into one work of art.

- The pieces of a collage overlap.

- The collection of images in a collage are all related to the same topic.

- The class collage will be on the topic of American diversity.

4 **Distribute and go over Student Handout 3.**

- Tell students that they will work in pairs to create four images or symbols for the collage. Explain that each pair's collage pieces will be assembled into a class collage that tells how five different groups of people have contributed to American society.

- Go over the directions on Student Handout 3. Answer any questions students have.

- Assign each pair of students one of the five major groups covered in the Student Edition.

- Distribute the drawing paper.

5 **Have pairs learn about their assigned group and plan their collage pieces.**

- Have student pairs read the section in the Student Edition that corresponds to their assigned group. Then have them complete the Reading Notes for that group.

- Afterward, have pairs brainstorm ideas for collage pieces that will show their group's settlement story and key contributions.

6 **Have student pairs create and cut out their collage pieces.** Monitor student work. Give students adequate time to complete their pieces.

7 **Have students share their collage pieces and finish their Reading Notes.**

- Organize the class for sharing collage pieces. Around the room, post signs with the name of one of the five groups on each sign. Have all pairs who were assigned the same group form one larger group near their sign. Direct them to display their collage pieces on a section of the wall, using pushpins or tape. (**Note:** Later, students will take their pieces down and add them to the class collage.)

- After students have displayed their collage pieces, give them five minutes to add any information to their Reading Notes that they learned from other pairs' collage pieces.

- Have students rotate to a new station and complete the Reading Notes for that group. Time students at each station and keep them moving along until they have visited all five stations.

8 **Assemble the class collage on a map of the United States.** Project a transparency of *Information Master 3: Outline of the United States* onto a large piece of butcher paper, and trace the outline of the United States onto the paper. Have students assemble their collage pieces within the borders of the United States and affix them using glue sticks. (**Note:** Depending on the size of your class, you may want to have students do this in teams or in stages.)

9 **Debrief the activity.** Ask students: *What questions do you have about the collage pieces that you see? Can you name one contribution from each group? What did you find out about the United States that you did not know before?*

10 **Have students read Sections 3.2–3.11 and the Summary in the Student Edition.** Tell them to check their responses on their Reading Notes after reading the text. Use Guide to Reading Notes 3 to check students' work.

Information Master 3

Reading Further: New York City: Layers of the Past

1 **Before class, prepare for the Reading Further activity.** Gather materials that will help your students research the original settlers of their own neighborhoods or towns. Materials could include classroom or library books, the names of local streets, and photographs or information on local monuments or festivals.

2 **Project *Transparency 3B: New Amsterdam.*** Make sure you cover the transparency title as students will guess the location of the image. Ask the following visual discovery questions to help students analyze the image carefully and make some predictions:

- What do you see in this image?

- What time period do you think this image shows? What clues might help you predict the time period? (*sailing ships, canoes, people's clothing*) (After students have had a chance to guess, tell them that the image shows a town around 1650, but don't tell them the name of the town.)

- Can you guess which large American city this town grew into?

3 **Now project *Transparency 3C: New York City, New York.*** Cover the transparency title.

- Ask students if they can identify the city in this picture.

- Identify the first image as New Amsterdam and the second image as present-day New York City. Tell students that they are looking at the southern end of Manhattan Island. Point out the Hudson River (left side of picture) and the East River (right side of picture).

- Remind students that they have been learning about the diversity of the United States. Tell students that New York City is one of the most diverse cities in the world. Ask: *When do you think New York City became so diverse? Do you think the small town of New Amsterdam had a diverse population? Why do you think that?*

4 **Have students read Reading Further 3 in the Student Edition.**

Transparencies 3B and 3C

5 **Assign students to pairs or small groups, and tell them that they are going to solve a "history mystery" about their own neighborhood.**

- Let students know that they are going to work as history detectives to find out where the original settlers to students' own neighborhoods (or towns) came from. Students will need to search for clues.

- To each pair or small group, hand out the materials you gathered before class. Give students about 10 minutes to do research. (**Option:** If you are willing to have the activity last longer, you can write on the board or on chart paper a list of resources to use to look for clues. The list could include street names, classroom or library books, conversations with community members, and local monuments and festivals. Then ask students to conduct research, possibly over a night or weekend, and return to class with their findings.)

6 **Have students open their Interactive Student Notebooks to Reading Further 3 and summarize the information they have gathered.**

Processing

1 **Have students turn to Processing 3 in their Interactive Student Notebooks.** Review the directions. As an example, read or sing this verse about Asian American immigrants:

> They came from Asia, across the ocean,
>
> They settled out west in California,
>
> They built a railroad across the nation,
>
> This land was made for you and me.

Then have students complete the assignment.

Assessment

Masters for the chapter assessment appear in the *Lesson Masters*. Answers appear below.

Big Ideas

1. A	4. B	7. A
2. D	5. C	8. A
3. D	6. B	9. D

Social Studies Skills

10. C	11. D	12. B	13. A

Show You Know

14. The bulleted points in the instructions can serve as a rubric for this item.

English Language Learners

During the Processing activity, rather than having students write song lyrics, have them draw a picture that represents the ethnic group they learned about. This will help students who have a limited vocabulary. Another possibility is to have students work with partners, sharing ideas and receiving help with vocabulary.

Students with Special Needs

Create a written summary of the collage pieces presented for each of the five assigned groups and hand it out to students. This will help them get all the necessary information into their Reading Notes. You can also give them extra time to complete the Reading Notes. Students will be able to participate in the activity without feeling pressure about time.

Enrichment

For the Reading Further research, ask students to explore in greater depth the group that first settled in their neighborhood. Students can create an in-class presentation, including visuals and text. Allow them to work individually or in pairs.

Enrichment Resources

LearnTCI

Have students find out more about economics and researching the economy of their state by exploring the following Enrichment Resources for *Social Studies Alive! Regions of Our Country,* at www.learntci.com.

Internet Connections These recommended Web sites provide useful and engaging content that enforces skills development and mastery of subjects within the chapter.

Enrichment Readings These in-depth readings encourage students to explore selected topics related to the chapter. You may also find readings that relate the chapter's content directly to your state's curriculum.

TeachTCI

For the teachers' resources listed below, click on Enrichment Resources for *Social Studies Alive! Regions of Our Country* at www.teachtci.com.

Biography Bank Hundreds of short biographies of notable people in history are available in PDF format for you to share with your students.

***Study Your State* Resources** Teaching directions and student activity pages (PDF format) will help you guide your students through researching their state.

Additional Reading Opportunities

The following fiction and nonfiction books offer opportunities to extend the content in this chapter.

Abuela by Arthur Dorros. Illustrations by Elisa Klevin. (New York: Penguin, 1991)

A little girl dreams that she and her abuela (grandmother) are flying above New York City. As the girl sees the sights of the city, she relates them to her grandmother's journey from her native land to the United States. This book is also available in Spanish, and Spanish translated into English. The translator for Spanish into English is Sandra Marulanda Dorros.

A Braid of Lives: Native American Childhood by Neil Philip, Ed. (New York: Clarion, 2000)

This book contains American Indians' recollections of their childhoods. Text accounts of poverty, schooling, ceremonies, and other facets of daily life are combined with black-and-white photographs.

In America (Minneapolis: Lerner, 2007)

This 16-book series features an extensive range of titles about the various ethnic groups in the United States. Each book features famous people, traditions, timelines, photographs, and other pertinent information about an ethnic group. Titles, which are composed of the ethnic name and then "In America," include *British, Filipinos, Russians, Italians, Irish, Pakistanis, Puerto Ricans, Japanese, Vietnamese, Salvadorans, Mexicans, Koreans, East Indians, Cubans, Chinese,* and *Canadians.*

Island of Hope: The Story of Ellis Island and the Journey to America by Martin W. Sandler. (New York: Scholastic, 2004)

From 1892 to 1954, Ellis Island served as the first point of entry for more than 12 million immigrants. Using actual accounts from immigrants, this book tells the story of why they came to the United States and discusses some of the problems they faced in their new home.

Journeys in Time: A New Atlas of American History by Elspeth Leacock and Susan Buckley. Illustrations by Rodica Prato. (Boston: Houghton Mifflin, 2001)

A history of the American people is told through stories of immigration and migration. The book begins with the Anishinabes (Chippewas) settling in the Great Lakes region and ends with a Vietnamese family escaping its war-torn country to find a new life in the United States. Twenty stories along with maps, illustrations, and pertinent facts will enable students to understand migration and settlement in the United States.

Kai's Journey to Gold Mountain: An Angel Island Story by Katrina Saltonstall Currier. Illustrations by Gabhor Utomo. (Tiburon: Angel Island Association, 2005)

For many years, Angel Island served as the main point of entry for Asians entering the United States. This is an account of a young Chinese boy's journey to the United States with his family.

Let It Shine: Stories of Black Women Freedom Fighters by Andrea Davis Pinkney. Illustrations by Stephen Alcorn. (New York: Harcourt, 2000)

The stories of ten women involved in civil rights are told in this text. Students learn how Harriet Tubman, Mary McLeod Bethune, Shirley Chisholm, and others fought for the rights of African Americans.

Silent Movie by Avi. Illustrations by C. B. Mordan. (New York: Atheneum, 2003)

The story of an Eastern European family's journey to New York City is told in black-and-white illustrations and minimal text, reminiscent of a silent movie. The strong visual images help students understand the difficulties that immigrants in the early twentieth century faced.

For each group of Americans, read and follow the directions.

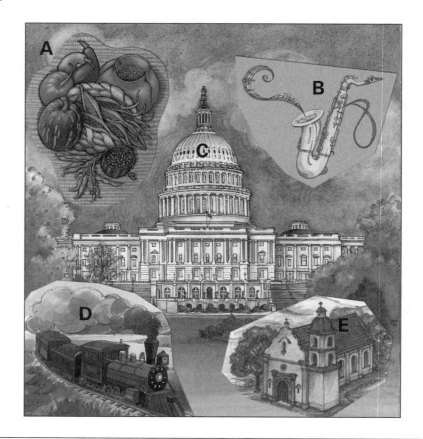

American Indians

Make a simple sketch to represent this group's settlement experience.

Write one sentence to describe this group's settlement experience.

Answers will vary.

Look at the collage. Write the letter of this group's contribution: _____A_____

Latinos

Make a simple sketch to represent this group's settlement experience.

Write one sentence to describe this group's settlement experience.

Answers will vary.

Look at the collage. Write the letter of this group's contribution: _____E_____

European Americans

Make a simple sketch to represent this group's settlement experience.

Write one sentence to describe this group's settlement experience.

Answers will vary.

Look at the collage. Write the letter of this group's contribution: _____C_____

African Americans

Make a simple sketch to represent this group's settlement experience.

Write one sentence to describe this group's settlement experience.

Answers will vary.

Look at the collage. Write the letter of this group's contribution: _____B_____

Asian Americans

Make a simple sketch to represent this group's settlement experience.

Write one sentence to describe this group's settlement experience.

Answers will vary.

Look at the collage. Write the letter of this group's contribution: _____D_____

A Train Tour of the Northeast

What are different parts of the Northeast like?

Overview

Students take a "train tour" to learn about the Northeast region of the United States. In the Preview activity, a Geography Challenge introduces students to the Northeast. Then, in a Writing for Understanding activity, groups of students sit on a "train" and listen to a tour guide while they view images of places in the Northeast. Through interactive experiences, students learn key concepts and facts about the Northeast. In Reading Further, students discover why Lowell, Massachusetts, was important to the economy of the Northeast and what life was like for factory workers there. Students conclude by writing a letter describing what they have seen on their tour. The writing activity serves as the Processing assignment for the chapter.

Objectives

Social Studies
- Categorize key elements of the economy, geography, government, history, and people of the Northeast.
- Use a map of the region to trace the route of a tour through the Northeast.
- Identify the advantages and disadvantages of democracy, mass production, and laws.
- Analyze working conditions in the textile mills of Lowell, Massachusetts.

Language Arts
- Gather information from an audio tour. (listening)
- Synthesize information into letter form. (writing)
- Conduct an interview. (speaking and listening)

Social Studies Vocabulary

peak, American Revolution, canal, lock, skyscraper, mass production, Declaration of Independence, United States Constitution, mill, wage

Materials

Social Studies Alive! Regions of Our Country

Transparencies 4A–4J

Interactive Student Notebooks

Lesson Masters
- Student Handouts 4A–4E
- Information Masters 4A–4D

CD 1, Tracks 1–12

Interactive Desk Map or large U.S. map

12-inch squares of aluminum foil

paper cups

small stones

Time Estimates

Preview: 45 min.

Writing for Understanding: 5 sessions (varying lengths)

Reading Further: 45 min.

Activity	Suggested Time	Materials
Preview • Connecting to Prior Knowledge • Building Background Knowledge: Geography Challenge • Developing Vocabulary	45 minutes	• *Social Studies Alive! Regions of Our Country,* Sections 4.1 and pages 50 and 51 • Transparency 4A • Interactive Student Notebooks • Student Handout 4A (depending on class size, 1 or 2 copies, cut apart) • Interactive Desk Map or large U.S. map
Writing for Understanding Taking a tour of the Northeast and writing a letter synthesizing information about the region	*Phase 1* 60-minute sessions (3) • Introduction and Tour Sites 1–3 • Tour Sites 4–7 • Tour Sites 8 and 9 (Steps 1–9)	• *Social Studies Alive! Regions of Our Country,* Sections 4.1–4.12 and Summary • Transparencies 4B–4J • Interactive Student Notebooks • Information Masters 4A–4C (1 transparency, plus 1 copy per group of 3, of each) • Student Handouts 4B–4D (1 copy of each per student) • CD 1, Tracks 1–12 • 12-inch squares of aluminum foil (1 per group of 3) • paper cups (1 per group of 3) • small stones (20 per paper cup)
	Phase 2 45-minute sessions (2) • Northeast chart (Steps 10 and 11) • Letter writing (Steps 12 and 13)	• Student Handout 4E (1 copy per student) • Information Master 4D (1 copy per student or 1 transparency)
Reading Further Experiential discovery of Lowell textile mills	45 minutes	• *Social Studies Alive! Regions of Our Country,* Chapter 4 Reading Further • Interactive Student Notebooks
Processing The letter-writing assignment serves as the Processing activity for this chapter.		
Assessment	30 minutes	• Chapter 4 Assessment, Lesson Masters • Chapter 4 Assessment, Digital Teacher Resources

Preview

1 **Preparing for the Preview:** Before class, make enough copies of *Student Handout 4A: Geography Challenge Cards* to give each pair one Geography Challenge card and have a few left over. (It is helpful to have a pool for students to pick from, in case other pairs are still using their cards.) Then cut out the cards. (**Note:** You may want to laminate the cards for future use.)

2 **Connecting to Prior Knowledge:** Introduce the Northeast region.

- Tell students that during the year, they will learn about five regions of the United States, starting with the Northeast. To help students see where the Northeast region lies within the country, hold up the Interactive Desk Map or display a large map of the United States and point out the region. Then have students look at the graphic organizer in Section 4.1 of *Social Studies Alive! Regions of Our Country.* Ask: *What states do you see on this map of the Northeast? What sites do you think you will see on a tour of this region? What do you want to learn about this region?*

- Project *Transparency 4A: The Northeast Region.* Explain that all the places shown in the collage are in the Northeast. Ask: *Can you identify or describe any of these places?* (Students may be able to name the Capitol in Washington, D.C.; the statue of Abraham Lincoln in Washington, D.C.; and New York City, which is labeled.) Briefly describe for students the places shown in the other pictures (a harbor on the northeastern coast, the rocky shore of Maine, a New England covered bridge).

- Tell students they will be taking a tour of important places in the Northeast. Explain that the dots on the graphic organizer in Section 4.1 show the places where students will stop on the tour. Have students open their Interactive Student Notebooks to Preview 4 and write about the place in the Northeast that they most want to visit. After they complete the page, discuss their responses.

3 **Building Background Knowledge: Geography Challenge**

- Assign students to mixed-ability pairs. Pass out one Geography Challenge question to each pair.

- Have students open their Student Editions to pages 50 and 51 and their Interactive Student Notebooks to Geography Challenge 4. Review the directions with students and model completing one question before pairs work independently.

- Monitor students' work, using the Guide to Geography Challenge 4, found at the end of this lesson. After a pair finishes a card, have both students raise their hands to indicate that they are ready for you to check their work. When necessary, instruct students to revise their answers. Remind pairs to exchange cards with other pairs until all students have completed all or most of the cards.

- Review the correct answers to the Geography Challenge with students. Have students again look at the maps of the Northeast region in the Student Edition as you discuss the answers.

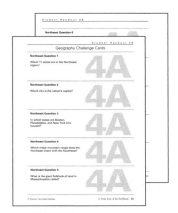

Student Handout 4A

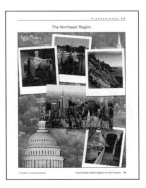

Transparency 4A

Reading Strategy: Recall Information

After completing the Geography Challenge, have students use one of the Extra Student Work pages at the back of the Interactive Student Notebook to record the main ideas they just learned. Then tell them to write continuously for a short period of time (no more than five minutes) everything they can remember about the geography of the Northeast.

4 **Developing Vocabulary:** Introduce key social studies terms—*peak, American Revolution, canal, lock, skyscraper, mass production, Declaration of Independence, United States Constitution, mill,* and *wage.*

- Discuss each term before beginning the activity, using methods described in *Solutions for Effective Instruction.*

- Review each term again with students as it appears in the activity reading, and encourage them to use it in their writing.

Writing for Understanding

Phase 1: Gathering Information

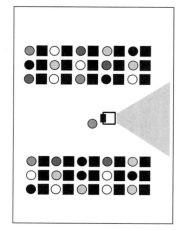

1 **Prepare for Phase 1 of the activity.** Assign students to mixed-ability groups of three and arrange the classroom according to the diagram. If necessary, prepare a transparency that shows students where they will sit. Make one copy of Information Masters 4A–4C for each group of three, as well as one transparency of each. Also make enough copies of Student Handouts 4B–4D to give one of each to every student at each of the three corresponding "train stops." (**Note:** The "tour" portion of this activity will take about three hour-long periods to complete—one period for Tour Sites 1–3, one period for Tour Sites 4–7, and one period for Tour Sites 8 and 9. You may want to prepare for only one session at a time.) Have aluminum foil squares, paper cups, and small stones ready before Tour Site 7.

2 **Introduce the activity.** Welcome students to the Northeastern Train Station as they enter the classroom. Then ask them to "board the train" and take their seats. Explain that shortly they will be taking a train tour of the Northeast region. Their tour guide's name is Ms. Mariner. Tell students that on the tour, they will see and learn about nine sites. At three of the sites, they will "get off the train" to examine visual and written information about the economy, geography, government, history, and people of the Northeast region.

3 **Play the first part of CD Track 1, "Introduction/The Northeast Coast."** This corresponds to the text of Section 4.1 in the Student Edition. Have students open their Student Editions and follow along.

4 **Pause the CD.** As a class, read aloud the three questions that Ms. Mariner asked. Tell students that they will need to listen for the answers to these questions throughout the activity. If desired, write the questions on chart paper so students can see them throughout the tour. Then have students turn to Reading Notes 4 in their Interactive Student Notebooks and read the directions. Tell them that they will use the map on this page to draw their route after they visit each site. Each time they fill in the map, ask them to suggest adjectives and key facts about the site. List these suggestions on chart paper and keep them there throughout the tour. (**Note:** Students will use this information to fill in a chart about the Northeast at Step 11.)

5   **For each site on the tour, project the corresponding transparency and play the corresponding track(s) on the CD.** The tour begins with *Transparency 4B: West Quoddy Head Lighthouse, Maine* and ends with *Transparency 4J: The Capitol Building, Washington, D.C..* The text of each CD track corresponds to a section of the Student Edition. Encourage students to read along in their Student Editions. To begin the tour, play the remainder of CD Track 1, which corresponds to Section 4.2. (**Note:** Throughout the activity, pause the CD as often as necessary to ensure student success.)

6   **After students visit each site, give them time to work on their Reading Notes.** Monitor student progress.

7   **To allow students to identify the advantages and disadvantages of democracy, mass production, and laws, respectively, have them "get off the train" three times.**

Transparencies 4B–4J

• For Tour Site 3, project *Transparency 4D:* Mayflower II, *Plymouth, Massachusetts* and play CD Track 3, "Democracy Takes Root at Plymouth." When the tour guide indicates that students should exit the train, pause the CD. Project a transparency of *Information Master 4A: Tour Site 3: Plymouth, Massachusetts* and pass out a copy of it to each group. Also pass out a copy of *Student Handout 4B: Tour Site 3: Plymouth, Massachusetts* to each student. Have groups read and follow the directions for the activity. After all groups have completed Step 3 of the directions on Information Master 4A, play the rest of CD Track 3. Then have students complete Step 4 of the directions. Afterward, discuss the responses students have written on Student Handout 4B.

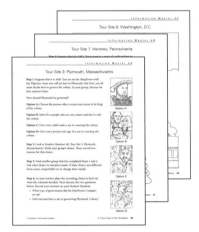

Information Masters 4A–4C

• For Tour Site 7, project *Transparency 4H: Chocolate Factory, Hershey, Pennsylvania* and play CD Track 7, "Hershey, Pennsylvania: A Town Built on Chocolate." When the CD track ends, project a transparency of *Information Master 4B: Tour Site 7: Hershey, Pennsylvania* and pass out a copy of it to each group. Also pass out a copy of *Student Handout 4C: Tour Site 7: Hershey, Pennsylvania* to each student. Give each group a pair of scissors, a 12-inch square of aluminum foil, and a paper cup holding 20 stones. Have groups read and follow the directions on the Information Master. Discuss the responses students write on their Student Handouts. In particular, address the pros and cons of wrapping machines, recording students' responses in a T-chart on the board. Point out that in many factories today, machines have taken over manufacturing tasks such as wrapping candy.

• At Tour Site 9, project *Transparency 4J: The Capitol Building, Washington, D.C.* and play CD Track 9, "Washington, D.C.: Our Nation's Capital." When the tour guide indicates that students should exit the train, pause the CD. Project a transparency of *Information Master 4C: Tour Site 9: Washington, D.C.* and pass out a copy of it to each group. Also pass out a copy of *Student Handout 4D: Tour Site 9: Washington, D.C.* to each student. Have groups read and follow the directions for the activity. Afterward, discuss the responses students have written on their Student

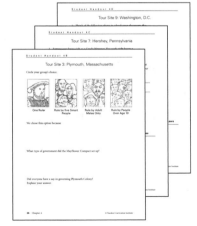

Student Handouts 4B–4D

Handouts. You may also want to discuss the question posed on the Information Master, "Are laws necessary?" To complete the Washington portion of the tour, play the rest of CD Track 9, then CD Track 10, "Our Government Buildings," and CD Track 11, "Our National Monuments."

8 After the tour, give students a few minutes to complete Reading Notes 4. Then have them check their Reading Notes and Student Handout answers against the Student Edition.

9 To wrap up the tour, play CD Track 12, "Summary," and have students follow along in the Student Edition. Hold a brief class discussion to make sure that students understand the answers to the three questions posed by Ms. Mariner at the beginning of the tour.

Phase 2: Organizing and Synthesizing Information

10 Prepare for Phase 2 of the activity. Make enough copies of *Student Handout 4E: Northeast Information Chart* for each student to have one.

11 Have students categorize key elements of the economy, geography, government, history, and people of the Northeast.

- Divide students into groups of four and assign each group one of the following topics related to the Northeast: economy, geography, government, history, or people.

- Pass out a copy of Student Handout 4E to each student. Give groups 10 minutes to review the adjectives and key facts that you recorded on chart paper. Then have groups fill in the appropriate information in their assigned row of the chart.

- When time is up, have each group present the information it included. Tell the other students to record this information on their own charts. Then ask if those students want to add anything to the row, and if it is appropriate, have everyone add it to his or her chart.

12 Tell students they will now write a letter describing their tour of the Northeast. Project *Information Master 4D: Writing a Letter About the Northeast* or pass out a copy of it to each student. Review the directions with students.

13 Debrief the activity. Have several students read their completed letters aloud. Then discuss the following questions:

For students who *do not* live in the Northeast, ask:

- What aspects of life in the Northeast did you most enjoy learning about?

- In what ways is life in the Northeast similar to life in your region of the country? In what ways is it different?

- Do you think you would like to live in the Northeast? Why or why not?

- If you were a tour guide like Ms. Mariner, what one site in the Northeast would you recommend that tourists visit? Explain.

Student Handout 4E

Information Master 4D

Writing Tip: Write Friendly Letters

Go over the parts of a friendly letter (including heading, salutation, body, and closing) and write them on a large sheet of paper. Encourage students to use this information as a resource for completing their letter-writing assignment.

For students who live in the Northeast, ask:

- What aspects of life in the Northeast did you most enjoy learning about?

- Did you learn anything new that surprised you? What was it? Why were you surprised?

- Do you like living in the Northeast? Why or why not?

- If you were a tour guide like Ms. Mariner, what one site in the Northeast would you recommend that tourists visit? Explain.

Reading Further: Lowell, Massachusetts: Factory Life

1   **Tell students that they are going to read about the thousands of women and girls who worked long, hard hours in cotton factories in Lowell, Massachusetts.** Explain that in the 1800s, Lowell was a major center of cotton production. In the factories, many women worked on looms to weave the thread into cloth. There were often 500 looms in one room, and workers typically worked on three looms at once. Some women were responsible for four looms at a time.

2   **To help students analyze the working conditions in the crowded Lowell mills, have them experience what it might be like to handle four looms each.** Assign students to mixed-ability groups of four. Have them arrange the room so that sets of four desks form a square, grouping the desks close together but leaving enough room for a student to step inside the square. Position all the squares of desks close to one another. On each desk, place six paper clips. Then have one student stand in each square for 30 seconds and try to connect the six clips on each of the four desks before time is up. Have the other students make machine noise to simulate the experience of being in a factory. If desired, also play some loud, distracting music.

3   **After all students have completed the activity, debrief the experience with the class.** Ask these questions:

- How would you describe your work environment?

- Were you able to connect the clips in all four sets? If not, why not?

- How did you feel trying to work on all four "looms" at once?

- How would you feel doing this task for 10 or 12 hours a day?

4   **Have students read all of Reading Further 4 in their Student Editions, independently or in small groups.**

5   **Ask students to open their Interactive Student Notebooks to Reading Further 4.** Have them read the directions. Then list on the board some topics students might cover in their interviews, such as the worker's age, his or her reasons for coming to Lowell, the type of work he or she does, the number of hours worked each day, or the conditions in the factory. Have students work in pairs to write interview questions. Then have them work individually to write the answers.

Assessment

Masters for the chapter assessment appear in the *Lesson Masters*. Answers appear below.

Big Ideas

1. B
2. B
3. A
4. D
5. D

6. C
7. C
8. A
9. B

Social Studies Skills

10. north

11. Annapolis, Harrisburg, Albany, Hartford, Providence, and Boston.

12. Vermont and Pennsylvania. They are the only two Northeast states that do not touch the Atlantic Ocean. (wording may vary)

Show You Know

13. The bulleted points can serve as a rubric for this item.

English Language Learners

For the Geography Challenge, match each English Language Learner with a student proficient in English. If necessary, provide instruction on how to read map legends, especially the circled star representing the nation's capital. Also be sure students understand terms used in the questions on the Geography Challenge Cards, such as *fishhook, Great Lakes,* and *harbor.*

Students with Special Needs

For the letter-writing activity, provide either a sample letter about the Northeast or a template that students can fill in. Also, allow students to use at least three, rather than seven, of the vocabulary words listed. Encourage them to refer to the glossary in the back of the Student Edition for help. For the Reading Further activity, provide a few sample interview questions and answers.

Enrichment

Have students research additional locations in the Northeast to create another tour of the region. Encourage them to create a map of the route, provide pictures of each location, and narrate (on audio or aloud in front of the class) interesting information about each location. Students may also want to write a paragraph on a large index card, describing each stop on the tour. Allow students to work individually or in groups and to share their completed tours with the class.

Enrichment Resources

LearnTCI

Have students find out more about the Northeast region by exploring the following Enrichment Resources for *Social Studies Alive! Regions of Our Country,* at www.learntci.com.

Internet Connections These recommended Web sites provide useful and engaging content that enforces skills development and mastery of subjects within the chapter.

Enrichment Readings These in-depth readings encourage students to explore selected topics related to the chapter. You may also find readings that relate the chapter's content directly to your state's curriculum.

TeachTCI

For the teachers' resources listed below, click on Enrichment Resources for *Social Studies Alive! Regions of Our Country* at www.teachtci.com.

Biography Bank Hundreds of short biographies of notable people in history are available in PDF format for you to share with your students.

***Study Your State* Resources** Teaching directions and student activity pages (PDF format) will help you guide your students through researching their state.

Additional Reading Opportunities

The following fiction and nonfiction books offer opportunities to extend the content in this chapter.

Empire State Building: When New York Reached for the Skies by Elizabeth Mann. Illustrations by Alan Witchonke. Photographs by Lewis Hine. (New York: Mikaya Press, 2006)

The story of constructing the Empire State Building is revealed through a mixture of fiction and nonfiction. The author covers the architecture, engineering, and construction of the skyscraper and includes profiles of the people who worked hundreds of feet above the ground to build the stunning structure. Original photographs and color illustrations support the text.

A Full Hand by Thomas F. Yezerski (New York: Farrar, Strauss and Giroux, 2002)

A nine-year-old boy in the 1800s learns how to navigate his father's canal boat in the Northeast. Information about locks and aqueducts is woven into the story. In a foreward, the author describes the importance of canals in the 1800s.

Grand Central Terminal: Gateway to New York City by Ed Stanley (New York: Mondo Publishing, 2003)

This narrative nonfiction book tells the compelling history of the planning, building, and effects of Grand Central Terminal from the mid-1800s to the present. Information about railroads is woven into the text. Maps, a timeline, and a glossary are included along with photographs.

Those Building Men by Angela Johnson. Illustrations by Barry Moser. (New York: The Blue Sky Press, 2001)

In this picture book, the author pays tribute to the contributions of African Americans, American Indians, and Asian and European immigrants to the construction of structures, such as the Erie Canal, the railroads, and skyscrapers, that adorn the American landscape. The role that women played in building such monuments is covered in an endnote.

Use the spaces below to answer the questions on the Geography Challenge Cards. Write complete sentences. Then, on the map, draw and label the feature that answers each question. Exchange your question with another pair of students until you have completed all the cards.

Question 1.   Which 11 states are in the Northeast region?

The 11 states in the Northeast region are Pennsylvania, Maryland, New York, New Jersey, Delaware, Vermont, New Hampshire, Connecticut, Rhode Island, Massachusetts, and Maine.

Question 2.   Which city is the nation's capital?

The nation's capital is Washington, D.C.

Question 3.   In which states are Boston, Philadelphia, and New York City located?

Boston is in Massachusetts. Philadelphia is in Pennsylvania. New York City is in New York.

Question 4.   Which major mountain range does the Northeast share with the Southwest?

The Appalachian mountain range runs through most of the Northeast.

Question 5.   What is the giant fishhook of land in Massachusetts called?

The giant fishhook of land in Massachusetts is called Cape Cod.

Question 6.   Which of the Great Lakes are in the Northeast?

Lake Erie and Lake Ontario are the two Great Lakes in the Northeast.

Question 7.   Which river empties into New York Harbor?

The Hudson River empties into New York Harbor.

Question 8. **Which river runs through the nation's capital?**

The Potomac River runs through the nation's capital.

Question 9. **Which river runs northeast from the Great Lakes?**

The St. Lawrence River runs northeast from the Great Lakes.

Question 10. **Which ocean lies east of the states in the Northeast?**

The Atlantic Ocean lies east of the states in the Northeast.

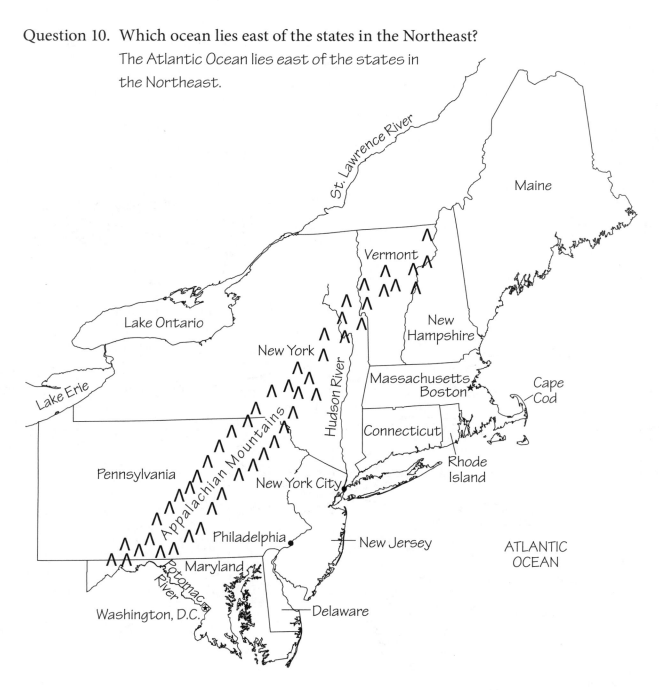

Your class is taking a train tour of the Northeast region. The tour will take you to nine locations. As you move from site to site, draw a line on the map to show your route. After visiting each site, draw a symbol or an image at that location to show what you learned there.

Students' symbols and images for each site will vary.

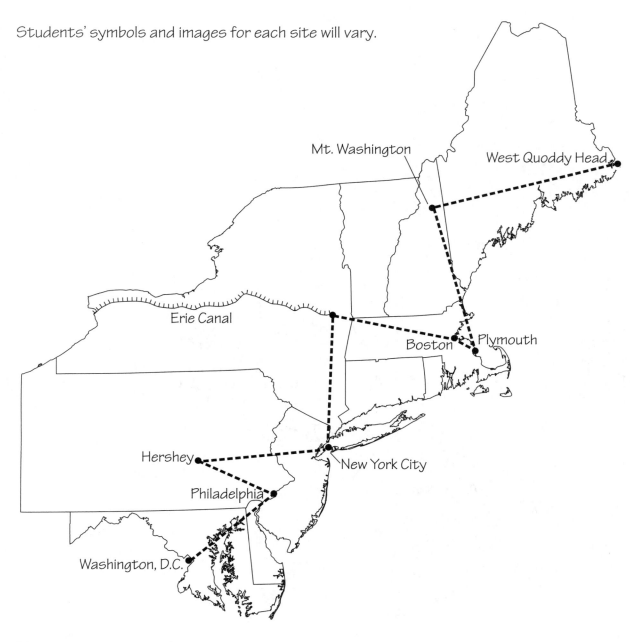

Population Density and Life in the Northeast

How do people live in the Northeast?

Overview

Students learn how population density in the Northeast affects the lives of the people who live there. During the Preview, students analyze an image of the United States at night. In an Experiential Exercise, students use their bodies and desks to simulate the population densities of the Northeast and several comparative locales. As they physically create the population density for each locale, they respond to a series of questions about how population density might affect people's lives. Afterward, students read and record notes about how life in the Northeast megalopolis differs from life in a small town. In Reading Further, students learn about some inventors and inventions that helped make the modern city possible. During the Processing activity, students create comic strips about life in the Northeast.

Objectives

Social Studies
- Simulate the population density of the Northeast and compare it with that of other regions of the United States.
- Evaluate the effect of population density on the lives of urban- and rural-dwelling northeasterners.
- Describe the relationship between inventions and changes in city life.

Language Arts
- Synthesize information from the reading into creative writing. (writing)

Social Studies Vocabulary

megalopolis, population density, pollution

Materials

Social Studies Alive! Regions of Our Country

Transparencies 5A and 5B

Interactive Student Notebooks

Lesson Masters
- Information Masters 5A and 5B

Interactive Desk Maps

Time Estimates

Preview: 30 min.

Experiential Exercise: 2 sessions (45 min. each)

Reading Further: 30 min.

Processing: 30 min.

Activity	Suggested Time	Materials
Preview • Connecting to Prior Knowledge • Developing Vocabulary • Building Background Knowledge	30 minutes	• Transparency 5A • Interactive Student Notebooks • Interactive Desk Maps
Experiential Exercise Exploring population density	*Phase 1* 45 minutes • Experiencing population density (Steps 1–7) *Phase 2* 45 minutes • Understanding how population density affects daily life (Steps 8–12)	• Information Master 5A (1 transparency) • Information Master 5B (1 copy) • *Social Studies Alive! Regions of Our Country,* Sections 5.1–5.8 and Summary • Interactive Student Notebooks
Reading Further Discovering inventions and inventors of the late 1800s and early 1900s	30 minutes	• *Social Studies Alive! Regions of Our Country,* Chapter 5 Reading Further • Transparency 5B • Interactive Student Notebooks
Processing Creating comic strips	30 minutes	• Interactive Student Notebooks
Assessment	30 minutes	• Chapter 5 Assessment, Lesson Masters • Chapter 5 Assessment, Digital Teacher Resources

Preview

1 Connecting to Prior Knowledge: Review with students the regions of the United States.

- Assign students to mixed-ability pairs and distribute an Interactive Desk Map to each pair.

- Ask students to point to each of the five regions of the United States on their Interactive Desk Maps. Have them identify the region in which they live. Ask them to recall what they learned about each region in Chapter 2.

Interactive Desk Map

2 Developing Vocabulary: Introduce key social studies terms—*megalopolis, population density,* and *pollution.*

- Discuss each term before beginning the activity, using methods described in *Solutions for Effective Instruction.*

- Review each term again with students as it appears in the activity reading, and encourage them to use it in their writing.

3 Building Background Knowledge: Introduce the Northeast as a densely populated part of the United States.

- Project *Transparency 5A: The United States at Night.* Ask partners to examine the image and respond to the questions on Preview 5 in their Interactive Student Notebooks.

Transparency 5A

- Afterward, debrief by discussing the Preview questions:

  - What do the bright areas on this photograph of the United States represent? What do the dark areas represent? *(The bright areas represent the lights that shine from the houses and businesses in populated areas. The dark areas are places where there are few lights. Few or no people live there.)*

  - In which half of the country do more people live, the East or the West? Why do you think this might be so? *(The eastern half of the United States is more settled. That is why there are so many more lights than in the western half. There are several reasons for this. One is that the Europeans who first came to the United States settled in the East, so there has been a longer time for settlement. A second reason is that there are huge areas in the West where it is hard for humans to live. Very high mountains and desolate stretches of desert cover large areas of the West.)*

  - There is a concentration of lights in the Northeast. Compare this image with the large U.S. map on your Interactive Desk Map, which shows some of the cities of the Northeast. Which large cities are bunched together along the Northeast coast of the United States? *(Some of the northeastern cities along the eastern seaboard are Washington, D.C.; Baltimore; Philadelphia; New York; and Boston. These are some of the most populated cities in the United States. More than 8 million people live in New York City alone. This region was the first to be called a megalopolis—a region of connected cities. That designation can be applied to other regions of the United States and to other places in the world. However, the Northeast megalopolis is a distinct place in many ways.)*

- Explain that, in this activity, students will closely examine population patterns in the Northeast and learn about how they affect people's lives there.

Experiential Exercise

Phase 1: Experiencing Population Density

1 **Prepare for Phase 1 of the activity.** Before class, make a transparency of *Information Master 5A: Table of Population Densities*. From a copy of *Information Master 5B: Population Density Props*, cut and assemble the 3-inch-tall "fourth grader," and cut out the paper square for use during the activity. (**Option:** Cut a paper rectangle the size of a student desk, from butcher paper, to use at Step 5.)

2 **Explain the purpose of the activity.** Tell students that this activity will give them a sense of just how densely populated the Northeast region is and how that might affect the lives of northeasterners.

3 **Ask students to set up the room for the activity.** Tell them to move 24 desks to the center of the room and then stand outside the desks, on the periphery of the classroom, as shown on the right.

4 **Project a transparency of Information Master 5A and ask students to simulate the population density of the United States.**

- Cover all but the first row of the table.

- Ask 30 students to sit in the 24 desks. Explain that the desks represent the land area of the entire United States—more than 3.5 million square miles—and that each of the 30 students represents 10 million people. More than 300 million people live in the United States today.

- Ask these questions: *How do you feel? What three words or phrases would you use to describe the population density of the United States?*

5 **Have students simulate the population density of the West and Northeast regions, and ask a series of debriefing questions.**

- Reveal the next two rows of the table.

- Ask seven students to occupy 8 desks on one side of the classroom. Tell them that they represent the population density of the West. Then ask five other students to occupy just one desk on the other side the classroom. (**Note:** Consider the safety aspects of this request. You may want to place a piece of butcher paper on the floor to represent the single desk.) Tell this group of students that they represent the population density of the Northeast. Use Information Master 5A to provide additional details.

- Ask the following questions:

  - How do you students in the West feel?

  - What three words or phrases would you use to describe the population density of the West?

  - How do you students in the Northeast feel?

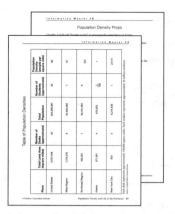

Information Masters 5A and 5B

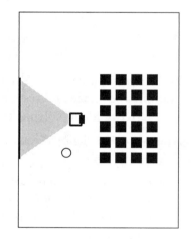

- What three words or phrases would you use to describe the population density of the Northeast?

- How does the population density of the West compare with that of the Northeast? Why do you think this is the case?

6 **Have students simulate the population density of Alaska and the New York metropolitan area, and ask a series of debriefing questions.**

- Reveal the fourth and fifth rows of the table. Tell students that the least densely populated state in the West is Alaska and that the New York metropolitan area is one of the most densely populated places in the country.

- Place four desks on one side of the room. Tape the 3-inch-tall "fourth grader" from Information Master 5B to the desk. Tell students that, to represent the population density of Alaska, we must use only a fraction of a whole fourth grader. Use Information Master 5A to provide additional details about the population density of Alaska.

- Ask these questions: *What do you think it would be like to have so much unpopulated space in your state? How do you think the population density of Alaska might affect life there?*

- Next, tape the paper square from Information Master 5B to the floor. Tell two students to try to sit on the paper square. (They will find this impossible; one student may think of sitting on the other's lap).

- Explain that the two students on the paper square represent the population density of New York City. This is one of the most densely populated places in the United States, with more than 8 million people. In New York City there are 27,110 people per square mile.

- Ask the two students these questions: *How do you feel? How does the population density of the New York metropolitan area compare with that of Alaska? With that of the West? With that of the Northeast?*

7 **Help students further compare the effects of population density on residents of Alaska and New York.** Ask these questions:

- Where do you think it is more expensive to purchase a home, Alaska or New York City? *(New York City is one of the most expensive places in the United States to purchase a home.)*

- Where do you think it is more expensive to park your car, Alaska or New York City? *(In Alaska, parking is free or inexpensive. In New York City, where space is limited, many car owners have to rent space to park a car.)*

- How might population density affect life in New York City or in other large cities in the Northeast, like Boston or Philadelphia?

Phase 2: Understanding How Population Density Affects Daily Life

8 **Prepare for Phase 2 of the activity.** In class, assign students to mixed-ability pairs.

9 **Introduce Chapter 5 in *Social Studies Alive! Regions of Our Country.*** Tell students that in this chapter, they will learn how life in the Northeast is affected by population density. Have students read Section 5.1.

10 **Introduce the graphic organizer at the bottom of Section 5.1.** Ask these questions: *What do you see? How might these buildings be a good way to evaluate life in the cities and rural areas of the Northeast?*

11 **Have students read Sections 5.2 and 5.3 in the Student Edition.** Discuss the concept of population density and how it looks on the map.

12 **Give directions for the reading assignment.**

- Ask students to open their Student Editions to Section 5.4 and their Interactive Student Notebooks to Reading Notes 5.

- Explain that partners will work together to compare life in rural and urban areas of the Northeast. Tell students that there are many differences between life in the Northeast megalopolis and life in a small town.

- Ask students to read Section 5.4, and have one partner record notes about life in the megalopolis and the other partner record notes about life in a small town. Afterward, have each partner share what he or she discovered.

- Repeat this process for Sections 5.5 through 5.8. Then have students read the Summary.

Reading Further: Inventing New Ways of Living

1 **Project *Transparency 5B: Historical Advertisement.*** Ask the following visual discovery questions to help students analyze the image and make predictions:

- What do you see in this image?

- What time period do you think these ads might be from? What clues might help you guess? (After students guess, tell them that these ads are from the late 1800s and early 1900s.)

- Why might these things have been advertised? (Students may guess correctly that these products were for sale in stores. Tell them that many of these things were brand-new inventions. Advertisements were one way for companies to introduce new products to people. Explain that students will be learning about some of the inventions that helped make the modern, densely populated city possible.)

- Can you guess which inventions helped make the modern city possible? What inventions do you think you will learn about?

Transparency 5B

Reading Strategy: Code Text

Have students cut sticky notes into four strips. Label each strip with one of the following symbols:

* = Information I already know

\+ = Information I didn't know

! = Amazing!

? = I'm confused

As students read Sections 5.4 through 5.8, have them code the text with the sticky notes to represent their reactions to the reading. They may then share their coding with their partner.

2 Have students read, independently or in small groups, Reading Further 5 in the Student Edition.

3 Have students open their Interactive Student Notebooks to Reading Further 5 and complete the page. Tell them to refer to their Student Editions when explaining how these inventions changed city life.

Processing

1 Have students turn to Processing 5 in their Interactive Student Notebooks. Review the directions for creating a comic strip about life in the Northeast. Have students complete the page. If time permits, have them share their work with the class.

Assessment

Masters for the chapter assessment appear in the *Lesson Masters*. Answers appear below.

Big Ideas

1. C

2. D

3. B

4. D

5. A

6. C

7. B

Social Studies Skills

8. Students should circle a long, narrow area that includes Boston, New York City, Philadelphia, and Washington, D.C.

9. New York

10. New Jersey

11. Rhode Island. It has a much greater population density, which contributes to more air pollution from cars, factories, and homes.

12. Pennsylvania has a much bigger area, so its people can be more spread out.

Show You Know

13. The bulleted points can serve as a rubric for this item.

English Language Learners

Have students draw their own cartoon for the Processing activity and then work with a partner to complete the dialogue between the two characters. Each student will guide the story of the cartoon but will receive help in phrasing and vocabulary from his or her partner to complete the cartoon.

Students with Special Needs

During the Processing activity, have students focus on only one of the topics: housing, employment, transportation, the environment, or recreation. Ask the student which topic he or she would like to focus on, and help the student make a decision. You may also give students more guidance about what happens in each frame of the cartoon. For example, the first frame shows the characters meeting, etc.

Enrichment

During the Reading Further activity, have students elaborate on their invention. Allow them to create a more detailed model, either on the computer or by hand. Then have them write a short essay to explain how the invention works and what it will do to make life easier for others. Allow students to display their inventions or present them to the class.

Enrichment Resources

LearnTCI

Have students find out more about economics and researching the economy of their state by exploring the following Enrichment Resources for *Social Studies Alive! Regions of Our Country,* at www.learntci.com.

Internet Connections These recommended Web sites provide useful and engaging content that enforces skills development and mastery of subjects within the chapter.

Enrichment Readings These in-depth readings encourage students to explore selected topics related to the chapter. You may also find readings that relate the chapter's content directly to your state's curriculum.

TeachTCI

For the teachers' resources listed below, click on Enrichment Resources for *Social Studies Alive! Regions of Our Country* at www.teachtci.com.

Biography Bank Hundreds of short biographies of notable people in history are available in PDF format for you to share with your students.

***Study Your State* Resources** Teaching directions and student activity pages (PDF format) will help you guide your students through researching their state.

Additional Reading Opportunities

The following nonfiction books offer opportunities to extend the content in this chapter.

Cities (series) by various authors (Edina, MN: Checkerboard Books, 2005–2007)

This series features information about the history, economy, government, and culture of major cities. Each book includes a timeline, glossary, and boldfaced terms. Titles include *Boston, Los Angeles, New Orleans,* and *New York.*

The Erie Canal: A Primary Source History of the Canal That Changed America by Janey Levy (New York: Rosen, 2003)

Students learn about the building and operation of the Erie Canal through primary documents, illustrations, and timelines. The book will help students understand the ways the Erie Canal impacted the industrialization of America.

New York, New York! The Big Apple from A to Z by Laura Krauss Melmed and Frané Lessac (New York: HarperCollins Children's Books, 2005)

This clever alphabet book features locations and popular sites in New York. Illustrations and information about each place make this a good resource for students.

Read Sections 5.4 through 5.8.
Record notes in the appropriate
spaces.

Life in the Northeast Megalopolis

5.4 Housing

Many people live in apartment buildings.

5.5 Employment

There are many different kinds of jobs in the city.

5.6 Transportation

City streets are crowded. It's hard to have a car in a city.
People walk or take buses, taxis, and subways.

5.7 Environment

Pollution is a big problem in cities because many things people do cause pollution.

5.8 Recreation

There are lots of different things to do in a city.

Life in a Small Northeastern Town

5.4 Housing

Many people live in houses with yards.

5.5 Employment

There are not as many different kinds of jobs in small towns.

5.6 Transportation

People need cars in rural areas.
Some people ride bikes.
There may be no public transportation in some places.

5.7 Environment

Pollution is less of a problem in small towns because there are fewer people to cause pollution.

5.8 Recreation

People in small towns have fun outdoors year-round.
They might go to the city for a day.

1. Briefly explain how these inventions changed city life.

Electricity changed city life in this way:

Possible answer: Electricity allowed people in cities to have lights in their houses. It also allowed them to take trolleys rather than walk.

The automobile changed city life in this way:

Possible answer: Cars allowed people to live far away but work in the city.

2. Draw a picture of something you could invent to solve one problem of living in a densely populated city. Look at the following list for ideas:
   - places to live
   - getting around
   - people and pollution

Drawings will vary. They should depict inventions that solve a problem of city life.

A Boat and Bus Tour of the Southeast

What factors have shaped the culture of the Southeast?

Overview

Students tour the Southeast region of the United States by boat and bus. In the Preview activity, a Geography Challenge introduces students to the region. In a Writing for Understanding activity, students listen to a tour guide and view images depicting life in the Southeast. At three of the tour sites, students engage in interactive experiences and learn key concepts and facts about the region. Finally, students write a letter about their excursions in the Southeast. In Reading Further, students meet the quilters of Gee's Bend and view some extraordinary quilts. The letter-writing activity serves as the Processing assignment for the chapter.

Objectives

Social Studies
- Apply map skills to locate nine important places in the Southeast.
- Use a map of the region to trace the route of a tour through the Southeast.
- Describe the major physical and human features of the Southeast.
- Identify the difficulties that early colonists faced in Jamestown, Virginia; some different southeastern musical traditions; and the ways in which life in America has changed since the civil rights movement.
- Hypothesize the impact of geographic location on art.

Language Arts
- Gather information from an audio tour. (listening)
- Synthesize information into letter form. (writing)

Social Studies Vocabulary

swamp, savanna, hurricane, mineral, strip mine, delta, bayou, petroleum, plantation, segregation, abstract

Materials

Social Studies Alive! Regions of Our Country

Transparencies 6A–6K

Interactive Student Notebooks

Lesson Masters
- Information Masters 6A–6D
- Student Handouts 6A–6F

CD 1, Tracks 13–27

dice

game pieces

poster paper

precut paper squares

Time Estimates

Preview: 45 min.

Writing for Understanding: 4 sessions (varying lengths)

Reading Further: 40 min.

Activity	Suggested Time	Materials
Preview • Connecting to Prior Knowledge • Building Background Knowledge • Developing Vocabulary	45 minutes	• *Social Studies Alive! Regions of Our Country* Section 6.1 and pages 86 and 87 • Transparency 6A • Interactive Student Notebooks • Student Handout 6A (depending on class size, 1 or 2 copies, cut apart) • Interactive Desk Map or large U.S. map
Writing for Understanding Taking a tour of the Southeast and writing a letter synthesizing information about the region	*Phase 1* 60-minute sessions (3) • Introduction and Tour Sites 1–3 • Tour Sites 4–6 • Tour Sites 7–9 (Steps 1–7) *Phase 2* 45-minute session • Letter-writing (Steps 8 and 9)	• *Social Studies Alive! Regions of Our Country*, Sections 6.1–6.10 and Summary • Transparencies 6B–6J • Interactive Student Notebooks • Information Masters 6A–6C (1 transparency, plus 1 copy per group of 3, of each) • Student Handouts 6B–6F (1 per student) • CD 1, Tracks 13–27 • dice (1 die per group of 3) • game pieces (paper, buttons, coins, or other items; 1 per student) • poster paper • Information Master 6D (1 transparency or 1 per student)
Reading Further Learning about the quilters of Gee's Bend and making a quilt	40 minutes	• *Social Studies Alive! Regions of Our Country,* Chapter 6 Reading Further • Transparency 6K • Interactive Student Notebooks • precut paper squares (24" x 24" recommended, 1 per student)
Processing The letter-writing assignment serves as the Processing activity for this chapter.		
Assessment	30 minutes	• Chapter 6 Assessment, Lesson Masters • Chapter 6 Assessment, Digital Teacher Resources

Preview

1   **Preparing for the Preview:** Before class, make enough copies of *Student Handout 6A: Geography Challenge Cards* to give each pair one Geography Challenge card and have a few left over. (It is helpful to have a pool for students to pick from, in case other pairs are still using their cards.) Then cut out the cards. (**Note:** You may want to laminate the cards for future use.)

2   **Connecting to Prior Knowledge:** Introduce students to the Southeast region.

- Tell students that the next region of the United States they will be learning about is the Southeast. To help students see where the Southeast region lies within the country, hold up the Interactive Desk Map or display a large map of the United States and point out the region.

- Have students look at the graphic organizer in Section 6.1 of *Social Studies Alive! Regions of Our Country.* Ask these questions: *What do you see? The dots on the map show the locations of places on the tour you are about to take. Where will you be going? How many states will the tour travel through? Which place on the tour are you most excited about visiting?*

- Project *Transparency 6A: The Southeast Region.* Ask students to examine the collage of Southeast images and then respond to the questions about which place in the Southeast they would most like to visit on Preview 6 in their Interactive Student Notebooks.

- Discuss students' responses. Tell students that in this lesson, they will be mapping features of the Southeast. Afterward, they will meet Mr. Davis, who will take them on a trawler (fishing boat), bus, riverboat, and motorboat tour of the Southeast so they can learn more about the region.

3   **Building Background Knowledge: Geography Challenge**

- Assign students to mixed-ability pairs. Pass out one Geography Challenge question to each pair.

- Have students open their Student Editions to pages 86 and 87 and their Interactive Student Notebooks to Geography Challenge 6. Review the directions with them. You may want to model the process for completing one question before you invite pairs to work independently.

- Monitor students' work. After a pair finishes a card, have both students raise their hands to indicate that they are ready for you to check their work. Use Guide to Geography Challenge 6, found at the end of this lesson, to check their responses for accuracy and thoroughness. When necessary, instruct students to revise their answers. Remind pairs to exchange cards until all pairs have completed most or all of the cards.

- Review with students the correct answers to the Geography Challenge. Have students look again at the maps of the Southeast region in their Student Editions as you discuss the correct answers.

Student Handout 6A

Interactive Desk Map

Transparency 6A

Reading Strategy: Create True/False Questions

After students have completed the Geography Challenge, ask them to write one or more True/False questions about the geography of the Southeast. You can collect the questions and use them to play a game as a quick review.

4 **Developing Vocabulary:** Introduce key social studies terms—*swamp, savanna, hurricane, mineral, strip mine, delta, bayou, petroleum, plantation, segregation,* and *abstract.*

- Discuss each term before beginning the activity, using methods described in *Solutions for Effective Instruction.*

- Review each term again with students as it appears in the activity reading, and encourage them to use it in their writing.

Writing for Understanding

Phase 1: Gathering Information

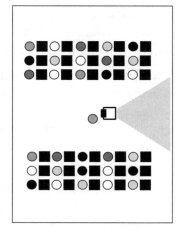

1 **Prepare for Phase 1 of the activity.** Before class, assign students to mixed ability groups of three and arrange your classroom according to the diagram. If necessary, prepare a transparency that shows students where they will sit. Make one copy of Information Masters 6A–6C for each group of three, as well as one transparency of each. Also make enough copies of Student Handouts 6B–6F to give one to every student at each of the three corresponding stops. (**Note:** The "tour" portion of this activity will take about three hour-long periods to complete—one period for Tour Sites 1–3, one period for Tour Sites 4–6, and one period for Tour Sites 7–9. You may want to prepare for only one segment at a time.)

2 **Introduce the activity.** When students enter the classroom, welcome them to the Southeast. Explain that shortly they will be taking a tour with their guide, Mr. Davis. Ask them to "step aboard the fishing trawler," a boat used in the fishing industry in the Southeast, and take their seats. Tell students that on this tour of the Southeast, they will see and learn about nine sites. They will stop at three sites to examine visual and written information to learn more about the history, economy, government, and people of the Southeast region.

3 **For each site on the tour, project the corresponding transparency and play the corresponding track(s) on the CD.** The tour begins with *Transparency 6B: Everglades National Park, Florida* and ends with *Transparency 6J: The Civil Rights Memorial in Montgomery, Alabama.* The text of each CD track corresponds to a section of the Student Edition. Encourage students to read along in their Student Editions. To begin the tour, play CD Track 13, "Introduction/Everglades National Park, Florida." Have students turn to Reading Notes 6 in their Interactive Student Notebooks and follow the directions. (**Note:** Throughout the activity, pause the CD as often as necessary to ensure student success.)

4 **After students visit each site, give them time to work on their Reading Notes.** Monitor students' progress.

5 **Students will stop three times to interact with station information and learn about European settlement, American musical traditions, and civil rights in the Southeast.**

Reading Strategy: Organize Information

Give each student a sticky note after each tour site is "visited." Have them write words or short phrases with the following information:

- place
- interesting/memorable information
- descriptive words
- new information

Students can attach the sticky notes to the corresponding pages in their Student Editions and use the notes to help them write letters about the Southeast in Step 8.

- For Tour Site 3, play CD Track 15, "Jamestown, Virginia: England's First American Colony" and project a transparency of *Information Master 6A: Tour Site 3: European Settlement at Jamestown, Virginia.* Also give each student a copy of *Student Handout 6B: The Survival Game* and *Student Handout 6C: Tour Site 3: European Settlement at Jamestown, Virginia.* Give each group one die and three game pieces. Have students read and follow the directions for the activity.

- For Tour Site 6, play CD Tracks 17 and 18, "Musical Memphis, Tennessee," and "The French Quarter in New Orleans, Louisiana." Project a transparency of *Information Master 6B: Tour Site 6: American Musical Traditions on a Mississippi Riverboat.* Also give each student a copy of *Student Handout 6D: Four Southeastern Musical Styles* and *Student Handout 6E: Tour Site 6: American Musical Traditions on a Mississippi Riverboat.* Give each group a pair of scissors. Then play CD Tracks 19–22, "Delta Blues: 'Low Life Street Blues,'" "Dixieland Jazz: 'Maple Leaf Rag,'" "Cajun: 'Les Barres de la Prison,'" and "Bluegrass: 'Salt Creek.'" Have students read and follow the directions for the activity.

- For Tour Site 9, play CD Track 25, "Montgomery, Alabama: Birthplace of the Civil Rights Movement," and project a transparency of *Information Master 6C: Tour Site 9: Civil Rights in Montgomery, Alabama.* Also give each student a copy of *Student Handout 6F: Tour Site 9: Civil Rights in Montgomery, Alabama.* Give each group a sheet of poster paper and some colored markers or crayons. Have students read and follow the directions for the activity. At the appropriate time, play CD Track 26, "'We Shall Overcome.'"

6 **After the tour, give students time to complete Reading Notes 6.** Then have them check their Reading Notes and Student Handout answers against the Student Edition.

7 **To wrap up the tour, play CD Track 27, "Summary." Have students follow along in their Student Editions.**

Phase 2: Synthesizing Information

8 **Tell students that they will now write a letter describing their tour of the Southeast.** Project a transparency of *Information Master 6D: Writing a Letter About the Southeast* or give one copy to each student. With students, read the directions for writing a letter, clarifying the requirements as needed. Then have students write their letters.

9 **Debrief the activity.** Have several students read their completed letters aloud. Then discuss the following questions:

For students who *do not* live in the Southeast:

- What aspects of life in the Southeast did you most enjoy learning about?

- In what ways is life in the Southeast similar to life in your region of the country? In what ways is it different?

Information Masters 6A–6D

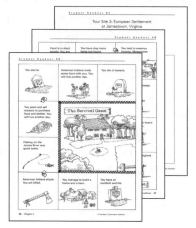

Student Handouts 6B–6F

Transparencies 6B–6J

- Do you think that you would like to live in the Southeast? Why or why not?

- If you were a tour guide like Mr. Davis, what one site in the Southeast would you recommend that tourists visit? Explain.

For students who live in the Southeast:

- What aspects of life in the Southeast did you most enjoy learning about?

- Did you learn anything new that surprised you? What was it? Why were you surprised?

- Do you like living in the Southeast? Why or why not?

- If you were a tour guide like Mr. Davis, what one site in the Southeast would you recommend that tourists visit? Explain.

Reading Further: The Quilters of Gee's Bend

1 **Prepare for the Reading Further activity.** Before class, assemble the materials that students will use to create their quilt squares. Precut enough paper squares (24" x 24" is recommended) to give one to each student. (**Option:** Give students a homework assignment to find at least one piece of paper or cloth to use in their quilts. It could be a worn piece of cloth that has meaning to the student or his or her family.) Decide ahead of time where students will assemble their quilts.

2 **Project** *Transparency 6K: Gee's Bend Quilts.* Cover the title and the text on each stamp. Ask the following visual discovery questions to help students analyze the images carefully and make some predictions:

- What do you see? Describe them in as much detail as you can. (If students don't recognize that these are stamps, reveal the postage on at least one of them.)

- What might the images on the stamps be? (Students may guess that they are paintings. After they have had a chance to respond fully, tell them that the images are of quilts. A quilt is a bedcover made of two layers of cloth that are filled with stuffing and stitched together.)

- Are you surprised to learn that these images are of quilts? Why or why not?

- Who do you think made these quilts? What might be so important about these quilts that they were put on stamps?

Transparency 6K

3 **Have students read Reading Further 6 in their Student Editions.** Allow them to read independently or in small groups.

4 **Have students open their Interactive Student Notebooks to Reading Further 6.**

- Tell students that they are going to make a quilt. Each student will make one square. Then the class will assemble the quilt. Remind students that the Gee's Bend quilts they have seen were influenced by people sharing ideas. Students will work in groups of three. They should share their ideas and help each other. The quilts they have seen are abstract in design. Students' quilt squares should also be in an abstract style.

- Give groups time to create their quilt squares.

- Have the class assemble the quilt.

- Ask students to examine the quilt, looking carefully at the materials and patterns in it. Ask: *Did geography affect the style of this quilt? How? Are there any elements of this quilt that relate to where we live? Would this quilt be the same or different if we lived in a different region? A city versus a town? How might it be the same or different?*

- Have students complete the questions on Reading Further 6 in their Interactive Student notebooks.

Assessment

Masters for the chapter assessment appear in the *Lesson Masters*. Answers appear below.

Big Ideas

1. D	6. A
2. D	7. B
3. B	8. A
4. C	9. D
5. C	10. A

Social Studies Skills

11. A

12. C

13. B

14. A

Show You Know

15. The bulleted points can serve as a rubric for this item.

English Language Learners

For the Processing assignment, allow students to write their letter with the assistance of another student. You may also want to allow students to write as much as they can in English and then work with a partner to improve sentence structure and vocabulary.

Students with Special Needs

Rather than having students write a letter, have them draw pictures with brief captions that address the questions that are asked. This will convey the same message but without the structure of a letter. Students might be more comfortable with drawing a picture and writing only a few words than with writing a whole letter.

Enrichment

Have students collect cloth and paper from the school community to create a quilt that is representative of their school. For example, students could collect art work from each grade level, or paper or cloth items with the school logo. Have students present the quilt to the principal as a gift from their class. Students could also take pictures of their quilt and create cards with a photograph of the quilt on the front.

Enrichment Resources

LearnTCI

Have students find out more about the Southeast region by exploring the following Enrichment Resources for *Social Studies Alive! Regions of Our Country,* at www.learntci.com.

Internet Connections These recommended Web sites provide useful and engaging content that enforces skills development and mastery of subjects within the chapter.

Enrichment Readings These in-depth readings encourage students to explore selected topics related to the chapter. You may also find readings that relate the chapter's content directly to your state's curriculum.

TeachTCI

For the teachers' resources listed below, click on Enrichment Resources for *Social Studies Alive! Regions of Our Country* at www.teachtci.com.

Biography Bank Hundreds of short biographies of notable people in history are available in PDF format for you to share with your students.

***Study Your State* Resources** Teaching directions and student activity pages (PDF format) will help you guide your students through researching their state.

Additional Reading Opportunities

The following books offer opportunities to extend the content in this chapter.

Hurricane Katrina Strikes the Gulf Coast by Mara Miller (Berkeley Heights, NJ: Enslow, 2006)
Interesting facts and accounts from survivors teach students about Hurricane Katrina and the destruction it caused in New Orleans and along the Gulf Coast.

The Long Gone Lonesome History of Country Music by Bret Bertholf (New York: Little, Brown & Co, 2007)
Students learn about the history of country music and how Nashville became "Music City, USA."

1607: A New Look at Jamestown by Karen Lange (Washington, D.C.: National Geographic, 2007)
This book shows Jamestown from the perspectives of the American Indians and the English settlers. It includes information from recent archaeological findings.

Team Moon by Catherine Thimmesh (New York: Houghton Mifflin, 2006)
This book focuses on the thousands of people at the Kennedy Space Center who helped land *Apollo 11* on the moon. Pages are filled with dramatic photographs of the moon and the space center, along with informational text.

Follow these steps to complete each card:
Use the spaces below to answer the questions on the
Geography Challenge Cards. Write complete sentences.
Then, on the map, draw and label the feature that answers
each question. Exchange your question with another pair
of students until you have completed all the cards.

Question 1.   Which 12 states are in the Southeast region?

The 12 states in the Southeast region are Arkansas, Louisiana, Mississippi,
Kentucky, Tennessee, Alabama, West Virginia, Virginia, North Carolina, South
Carolina, Georgia, and Florida.

Question 2.   Which states in the Southeast do not have coastlines?

Arkansas, Tennessee, Kentucky, and West Virginia do not have coastlines.

Question 3.   What are the flatlands called that cover much of the coastlines of
Mississippi, Alabama, and Florida?

The flatlands along the coasts of Mississippi, Alabama, and Florida are called
the Gulf Coastal Plain.

Question 4.   What are the flatlands called that cover much of the coastlines of Georgia,
North Carolina, and South Carolina?

The flatlands along the coasts of Georgia, North Carolina, and South Carolina
are called the Atlantic Coastal Plain.

Question 5.   Which major port city is in Alabama?

Mobile is a major port city in Alabama.

Question 6.   What major mountain range is located in the northeastern area of this
region?

The major mountain range in the northeastern area of this region is the
Appalachian Mountains.

Question 7.   What body of water is south of New Orleans?

The Gulf of Mexico is south of New Orleans.

Question 8. **Which major port cities are in Florida?**

The major port cities of Tampa, Miami, Jacksonville, and Pensacola are in Florida.

Question 9. **If you wanted to travel by canoe from Kentucky to Louisiana, which major river could you use?**

You could use the Mississippi River to travel from Kentucky to Louisiana.

Question 10. **Which three national parks could you visit if you traveled to Arkansas, Tennessee, and Virginia?**

You could visit Hot Springs National Park, Great Smoky Mountains National Park, and Shenandoah National Park.

Your class is taking a tour of the Southeast region.
The tour will take you to nine locations. As you move
from site to site, draw a line on the map to show your route.
After visiting each site, draw a symbol or an image at each
location to show what you learned there.

Students' symbols and images for each site will vary.

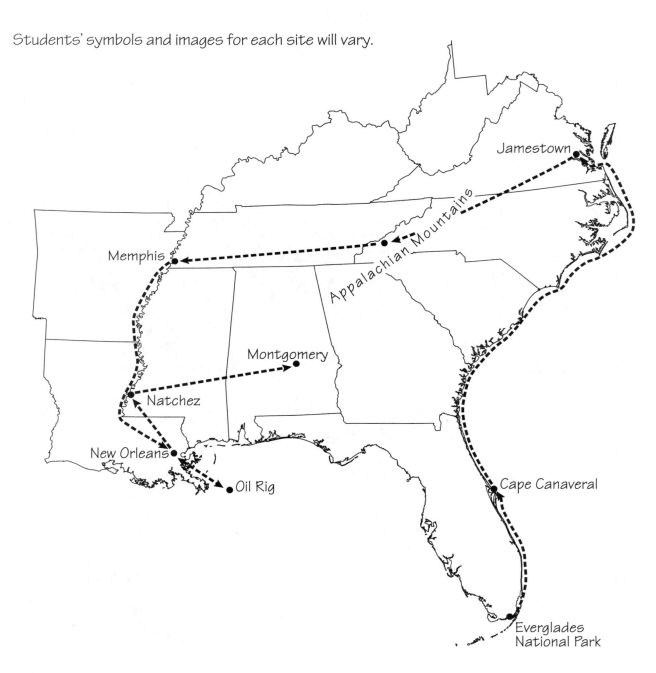

The Effects of Geography on Life in the Southeast

How has geography helped shape daily life in the Southeast?

Overview

Students learn how geography affects life in the Southeast region. In the Preview, students explore how geography affects people's choices. In a Social Studies Skill Builder, students look at maps and answer questions about climate, elevation, natural resources, and bodies of water. Students then hypothesize and read about the effects of geography on life in the Southeast. In Reading Further, students explore the effects of Hurricane Andrew on Florida. In a Processing activity, they create illustrations that show how geography affects life in their own community.

Objectives

Social Studies

- Interpret geographic information from special-purpose maps and images of the Southeast.

- Hypothesize the effects of geography and read to confirm or correct.

- Report on the effects of Hurricane Andrew on Florida.

- Apply what has been learned by identifying the effects of geography in their own community.

Language Arts

- Summarize ideas as written hypotheses. (writing)

Social Studies Vocabulary

foothills, navigable, fall line, natural resource, industry, agriculture, floodplain, tornado

Materials

Social Studies Alive! Regions of Our Country

Transparencies 7A–7H

Placards 7A–7F

Interactive Student Notebooks

Lesson Masters

- Student Handout 7

Time Estimates

Preview: 30 min.

Social Studies Skill Builder: 60 min.

Reading Further: 30 min.

Processing: 30 min.

Activity	Suggested Time	Materials
Preview • Connecting to Prior Knowledge • Building Background Knowledge • Developing Vocabulary	30 minutes	• *Social Studies Alive! Regions of Our Country*, Section 7.1 • Transparency 7G • Interactive Student Notebooks • Student Handout 7 (1 per group)
Social Studies Skill Builder Conducting a geographic investigation	60 minutes • Investigating the effects of geography on the Southeast (Steps 1–4)	• *Social Studies Alive! Regions of Our Country*, Sections 7.2–7.7 • Transparencies 7A–7F • Interactive Student Notebooks • Placards 7A–7F (2 sets)
Reading Further Exploring the effects of Hurricane Andrew	30 minutes	• *Social Studies Alive! Regions of Our Country*, Chapter 7 Reading Further • Transparency 7H • Interactive Student Notebooks
Processing Writing a letter	30 minutes	• *Social Studies Alive! Regions of Our Country*, Chapter 7 Summary • Interactive Student Notebooks
Assessment	30 minutes	• Chapter 7 Assessment, Lesson Masters • Chapter 7 Assessment, Digital Teacher Resources

Preview

1 Preparing for the Preview: Before class, assign students to small groups. Then make enough copies of *Student Handout 7: Analyzing Three Geography Scenes* to give one copy to each group.

2 Connecting to Prior Knowledge: Help students understand the ways in which geography influences people's lives.

- Project *Transparency 7G: Three Geography Scenes*. (**Note:** This transparency was placed at the end of the series of transparencies so that Placards 7A–7F correspond to Transparencies 7A–7F.)

- Distribute one copy of Student Handout 7 to each group.

- Lead students through the four steps on the handout, revealing the scenes on the transparency, one at a time.

- At Step 3, have students work independently to complete Preview 7 in their Interactive Student Notebooks.

- When they have completed the page, lead a discussion about how geography influences everything, from clothing choices to the activities people do in their spare time.

3 Building Background Knowledge: Introduce the geography of the Southeast.

- Tell students that in this lesson, they will learn about the effects of geography on life in the Southeast. Have them read Section 7.1 in *Social Studies Alive! Regions of Our Country*.

- Have students examine the graphic organizer in Section 7.1. Ask: *What do you see? What things in the image relate to the geography of the Southeast? How do you think geography might affect life in the Southeast?*

4 Developing Vocabulary: Introduce key social studies terms—*foothills, navigable, fall line, natural resource, industry, agriculture, floodplain,* and *tornado.*

- Discuss each term before beginning the activity, using methods described in *Solutions for Effective Instruction*.

- Review each term again with students as it appears in the activity reading and encourage them to use it in their writing.

Social Studies Skill Builder

1 Prepare for the activity. Before class, post both sets of *Placards 7A–7F: Geography Investigations* about 3 feet apart on the classroom walls. Assign students to mixed-ability pairs. Arrange the desks so that partners sit side by side and everyone faces the front of the classroom.

2 Help students interpret geographic information from special-purpose maps and images of the Southeast. Have students open their Interactive Student Notebooks to Reading Notes 7, and model how to complete the first page.

Student Handout 7

Transparency 7G

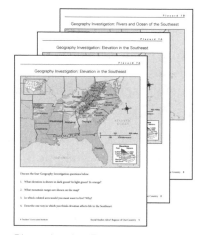

Placards 7A–7F

- Project *Transparency 7A: Geography Investigation: Elevation in the Southeast.* Tell students that in this activity, they will take the role of geographers investigating the question, *How does geography affect life in the Southeast?* Tell them that maps like this one will be especially helpful as they try to answer this important question.

- Review the Reading Notes directions with students.

- Ask pairs to complete Step 1 of the Reading Notes by finding the feature in the Reading Notes illustration that most relates to the projected map. Direct students to draw an arrow from the corresponding placard box in their Reading Notes to this feature.

- Ask volunteers to answer the first Geography Investigation question on the transparency. Ask one volunteer to point out the parts of the map that helped in answering the question. Repeat this step for Questions 2 and 3.

- Ask students to write a hypothesis (an educated guess) for Question 4 under Step 2 of their Reading Notes. Discuss their hypotheses.

- With students, read aloud Section 7.2 of the Student Edition. Have students complete Steps 3 and 4 of their Reading Notes.

- Point out the placards posted on the classroom walls and explain that students will circulate around the classroom with their partner and complete the rest of their Reading Notes using the correspnding placards.

3 **Have students complete their Reading Notes for the remaining sections.** Have pairs examine the remaining placards and read the corresponding sections of the Student Edition. To ensure that students understand the directions, check their answers after they complete one section of their Reading Notes on their own. Tell pairs that when they finish all the notes for each topic, they should raise their hands for you to check their work. Use Guide to Reading Notes 7 to evaluate their responses.

4 **After students have completed their Reading Notes, project *Transparencies 7B–7F: Geography Investigations.*** Discuss students' conclusions about each geographic influence.

Reading Further: Hurricane Andrew

1 **Project *Transparency 7H: Satellite Image of Hurricane Andrew.*** Ask the following visual discovery questions to help students analyze the image carefully and make some predictions:

- What do you see? Try to describe it in as much detail as you can.

- Can you guess what this photograph shows? (After gathering guesses, let students know that this is a photograph of a hurricane.)

- From where do you think this image was taken? (This is a satellite image, taken from space.)

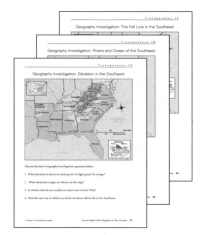

Transparencies 7A–7F

Vocabulary Development: Create Word Webs

As students read each section, have them create a word web for each social studies vocabulary term. Around each term, they should write characteristics or words that describe the term and draw a picture that illustrates it. Below each word web, students should use the term in a sentence.

Transparency 7H

- What landmass do you see in the upper left corner of the image? Hint: You are looking at part of a U.S. state; can you guess which one? (Florida)

- In the photograph, the hurricane is over water. What effect do you think this storm will have when it reaches land?

2   **Have students read Reading Further 7 in the Student Edition.** Allow them to read independently or in small groups.

3   **Have students report on the effects of Hurricane Andrew on Florida.** Ask students to open their Interactive Student Notebooks to Reading Further 7. Have them read the directions. Answer any questions they might have. Allow students to work in pairs to write and answer questions. Have students work individually to write their articles.

Processing

1   **Read aloud the Summary in the Student Edition.**

2   **Have students complete Processing 7 in their Interactive Student Notebooks to show the effects of geography where they live.** If time permits, let them share their illustrations with their classmates.

Assessment

Masters for the chapter assessment appear in the *Lesson Masters*. Answers appear below.

Big Ideas

1. D	4. B	7. A
2. B	5. C	8. D
3. C	6. A	9. D

Social Studies Skills

10. Florida

11. West Virginia

12. on the Coastal Plain

Show You Know

13. The bulleted points can serve as a rubric for this item.

> **Writing Tip: Brainstorm**
>
> Before students complete the Processing assignment, brainstorm with the class some possible effects of geography in your area. Make a list of students' ideas on the board.

English Language Learners

During the Reading Further activity, have students work with a partner to write the questions that a reporter might ask. To help students gain a clear understanding of the types of questions that are usually asked in an interview, find a newspaper article of someone being interviewed after surviving a disaster. With students, read the article so that they may better understand the types of questions reporters ask. After students write their own interview questions, help them formulate their ideas about answers (verbally or as a prewriting exercise) before proceeding with the activity.

Students with Special Needs

For the Processing activity, help students choose the three geography topics. Students may be able to fill in the section titled "Geography in My Area" on their own, but allow them to work with a partner to complete the section titled "Effects of Geography in My Area." Alternatively, you could send this activity home with students as a homework assignment to be completed with parental support. Students should be able to create the illustrations independently, once they understand the concepts.

Enrichment

Have students choose an example of how weather has affected life in their region (the more dramatic, the better). Then have them research this example and make a poster for presentation. The poster should include pictures (before and after), with descriptions of how life in the region has been affected. Students may also want to interview people who witnessed the event, to gather some personal examples of how life may have changed, for the better or for worse.

Enrichment Resources

LearnTCI

Have students find out more about the geography of the Southeast by exploring the following Enrichment Resources for *Social Studies Alive! Regions of Our Country,* at www.learntci.com.

Internet Connections These recommended Web sites provide useful and engaging content that enforces skills development and mastery of subjects within the chapter.

Enrichment Readings These in-depth readings encourage students to explore selected topics related to the chapter. You may also find readings that relate the chapter's content directly to your state's curriculum.

TeachTCI

For the teachers' resources listed below, click on Enrichment Resources for *Social Studies Alive! Regions of Our Country* at www.teachtci.com.

Biography Bank Hundreds of short biographies of notable people in history are available in PDF format for you to share with your students.

***Study Your State* Resources** Teaching directions and student activity pages (PDF format) will help you guide your students through researching their state.

Additional Reading Opportunities

The following nonfiction books offer opportunities to extend the content in this chapter.

The Fury of Hurricane Andrew by Karen Bush Gibson (New York: Mitchell Lane Publishers, 2005)
Dramatic personal accounts and photographs show students the devastation that Hurricane Andrew caused in southern Florida and Louisiana.

J. Rooker, Manatee by Jan Haley (Bemidji, MN: Focus Publishing, 2002)
Students learn about the true story of an injured manatee rescued by environmental advocates and efforts to preserve the natural beauty of Florida.

Miami Metrozoo by Sherrie Avery (New York: Rosen, 2003)
Students take a photo tour of this Miami-area zoo, learning about exotic animals and beautiful foliage. They also learn about the impact of Hurricane Andrew.

National Park and *Great Smoky Mountains National Park. National Parks* (series) by John Hamilton (Edina, Minnesota: Abdo, 2005)
This series features photographs, maps, and diagrams that highlight the ecosystems, geology, geography, and animals of our national parks. Titles include *Everglades National Park* and *Great Smoky Mountains National Park.*

How does geography affect life in the Southeast? Investigate for yourself.
For each placard, follow the four steps in the corresponding box on the
following pages.

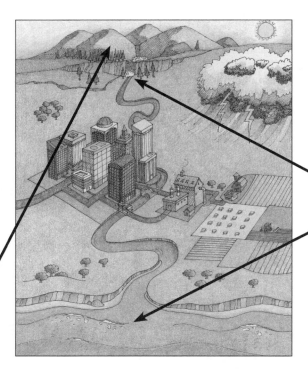

Placement of lines may vary.

Placard 7A: Geography Investigation: Elevation in the Southeast

Step 1: Draw an arrow from this box to the geography feature in
the illustration that best matches the map on the wall.

Step 2: Write your hypothesis (educated guess) to Geography Investigation
Question 4.
*Answers will vary but may mention the effects of natural resources on people's
occupations.*

Step 3: Read Section 7.2 in *Social Studies Alive! Regions of Our Country*.
Is your hypothesis mentioned in the book? Circle *yes* or *no*.   Yes   No

Step 4: Write one effect that elevation has on the Southeast region.
*Possible answer: Elevation affects climate. It is colder in the highlands than in the
lowlands. The temperature influences which plants can be grown.*

Placard 7B: Geography Investigation: Rivers and Ocean of the Southeast

Step 1: Draw an arrow from this box to the geography feature in the illustration that best matches the map on the wall.

Step 2: Write your hypothesis (educated guess) to Geography Investigation Question 4. *Answers will vary but may mention the effects of rivers and the ocean on transportation and natural resources.*

Step 3: Read Section 7.3 in *Social Studies Alive! Regions of Our Country.* Is your hypothesis mentioned in the book? Circle *yes* or *no*.   Yes   No

Step 4: Write one effect that the rivers and the ocean have on the Southeast region.
Possible answer: The people of the Southeast use the rivers and the ocean for recreational activities like boating, fishing, and taking cruises.

Placard 7C: Geography Investigation: The Fall Line in the Southeast

Step 1: Draw an arrow from this box to the geography feature in the illustration that best matches the map on the wall.

Step 2: Write your hypothesis (educated guess) to Geography Investigation Question 4.
Answers will vary but may mention the effects of the fall line on transportation.

Step 3: Read Section 7.4 in *Social Studies Alive! Regions of Our Country.* Is your hypothesis mentioned in the book? Circle *yes* or *no*.   Yes   No

Step 4: Write one effect that the fall line has on the Southeast region.
Possible answer: Trading posts and power from falling water at the fall line helps towns in the Piedmont grow into cities.

Placement of lines may vary.

Placard 7D: Geography Investigation: Natural Resources of the Southeast

Step 1: Draw an arrow from this box to the geography feature in the illustration that best matches the map on the wall.

Step 2: Write your hypothesis (educated guess) to Geography Investigation Question 4.

Answers will vary but may mention the effects of natural resources on people's occupations.

Step 3: Read Section 7.5 in *Social Studies Alive! Regions of Our Country*.

Is your hypothesis mentioned in the book? Circle *yes* or *no*.   Yes   No

Step 4: Write one effect that natural resources have on the Southeast region

Possible answer: Many people have jobs, such as making products from wood, because of the region's large forests.

Placard 7E: Geography Investigation: Growing Seasons in the Southeast

Step 1: Draw an arrow from this box to the geography feature in the illustration that best matches the map on the wall.

Step 2: Write your hypothesis (educated guess) to Geography Investigation Question 4.

Answers will vary but may mention the effects of the lengthy growing season on types and numbers of crops grown.

Step 3: Read Section 7.6 in *Social Studies Alive! Regions of Our Country.*
Is your hypothesis mentioned in the book? Circle *yes* or *no.*   Yes   No

Step 4: Write one effect that the lengthy growing season has on the Southeast region.

Possible answer: The warm climate makes the Southeast a good place for raising crops and animals.

Placard 7F: Geography Investigation: Dangerous Weather in the Southeast

Step 1: Draw an arrow from this box to the geography feature in the illustration that best matches the map on the wall.

Step 2: Write your hypothesis (educated guess) to Geography Investigation Question 4.

Answers will vary but may mention the effects of tornados, hurricanes and floods on housing and building construction.

Step 3: Read Section 7.7 in *Social Studies Alive! Regions of Our Country.*
Is your hypothesis mentioned in the book? Circle *yes* or *no.*   Yes   No

Step 4: Write one effect that weather events have on the Southeast region.
Possible answer: Floods, hurricanes, and tornados can destroy homes and crops.

A Crop Duster Tour of the Midwest

Why do we call the Midwest "America's Heartland"?

Overview

Students tour the Midwest region of the United States. In the Preview, a Geography Challenge introduces students to the Midwest. In a Writing for Understanding activity, students listen to a tour guide and view images of the Midwest. Through interactive experiences, students learn key concepts and facts about the region. Then students use their notes to write a letter about their excursions in the Midwest. In Reading Further, students learn what life was like in one Midwestern city—Detroit, Michigan—during World War II. The writing activity serves as the Processing assignment for this chapter.

Objectives

Social Studies

- Describe the major physical and human features of the Midwest.
- Apply map skills to locate nine important sites in the Midwest.
- Use a map of the region to trace the route of a tour through the Midwest.
- Categorize key elements of the economy, geography, transportation, history, and people of the Midwest over time.
- Write about Detroit during World War II from one of two points of view.

Language Arts

- Gather information from an audio tour. (listening)
- Synthesize information into letter form. (writing)

Social Studies Vocabulary

frontier, prairie, fertile, livestock, feedlot, meatpacking, reservation, assembly line, transportation hub

Materials

Social Studies Alive! Regions of Our Country

Transparencies 8A–8K

Interactive Student Notebooks

Lesson Masters

- Student Handouts 8A–8H
- Information Masters 8A–8D

CD 1, Tracks 28–39

large sheets of paper

Time Estimates

Preview: 45 min.

Writing for Understanding: 5 sessions (varying lengths)

Reading Further: 30 min.

Activity	Suggested Time	Materials
Preview • Connecting to Prior Knowledge • Building Background Knowledge: Geography Challenge • Developing Vocabulary	45 minutes	• *Social Studies Alive! Regions of Our Country,* Section 8.1, pages 118, 119 • Transparency 8A • Interactive Student Notebooks • Student Handout 8A (depending on class size, 1 or 2 copies, cut apart)
Writing for Understanding Taking a tour of the Midwest and writing a letter synthesizing information about the region	*Phase 1* 60-minute sessions (3) • Introduction and Tour Sites 1–3 • Tour Sites 4–6 • Tour Sites 7–9 (Steps 1–8) *Phase 2* 45-minute sessions (2) • Midwest chart (Steps 9 and 10) • Letter-writing (Steps 11 and 12)	• *Social Studies Alive! Regions of Our Country,* Sections 8.1–8.10 and Summary • Transparencies 8B–8J • Interactive Student Notebooks • Information Masters 8A–8C (1 copy per group of 3, plus 1 transparency of each) • Student Handouts 8B–8D and 8F (1 of each per student) • Student Handout 8E (25 copies per group of 6) • Student Handout 8G (1 per group of 6) • CD 1, Tracks 28–39 • large sheets of paper • Student Handout 8H (1 per student) • Information Master 8D (1 per student or 1 transparency)
Reading Further Learning about Detroit in World War II	30 minutes	• *Social Studies Alive! Regions of Our Country,* Chapter 8 Reading Further • Transparency 8K • Interactive Student Notebooks
Processing The letter-writing assignment serves as the Processing activity for this chapter.		• Interactive Student Notebooks
Assessment	30 minutes	• Chapter 8 Assessment, Lesson Masters • Chapter 8 Assessment, Digital Teacher Resources

Preview

1   **Preparing for the Preview:** Before class, make enough copies of *Student Handout 8A: Geography Challenge Cards* to give each pair one Geography Challenge card and have a few left over. (It is helpful to have a pool for students to pick from, in case other pairs are still using their cards.) Then cut out the cards. (**Note:** You may want to laminate the cards for future use.)

2   **Connecting to Prior Knowledge:** Introduce students to the Midwest region.

   - Tell students that the next region of the United States they will be learning about is the Midwest.

   - Project *Transparency 8A: The Midwest Region*. Ask students to examine the collage of Midwest images and answer the questions on Preview 8 in their Interactive Student Notebooks.

   - Discuss students' responses and tell them that in this activity they will be mapping features of the Midwest. Afterward, students will take a plane tour of the Midwest to learn more about the region.

   - Have students examine the graphic organizer in Section 8.1 of *Social Studies Alive! Regions of Our Country*. Ask these questions: *What do you see? Where will you be going on your tour? How many states will the tour travel through? Which place on the tour are you most excited about visiting?*

3   **Building Background Knowledge: Geography Challenge**

   - Assign students to mixed-ability pairs. Pass out one Geography Challenge question to each pair.

   - Have students open their Student Editions to pages 118 and 119 and their Interactive Student Notebooks to Geography Challenge 8. Review the directions with students and model completing one question before pairs work independently.

   - Monitor students' work, using Guide to Geography Challenge 8, found at the end of the lesson. After a pair finishes a card, have both students raise their hands to indicate that they are ready for you to check their work. When necessary, instruct students to revise their answers. Remind pairs to exchange cards with other pairs until all students have completed all or most of the cards.

   - Review with students the correct answers to the Geography Challenge. Have students again look at the maps of the Midwest region, on pages 118 and 119 of the Student Edition, as you discuss the answers.

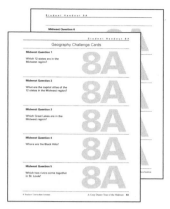

Student Handout 8A

Transparency 8A

4 Developing Vocabulary: Introduce key social studies terms—*frontier, prairie, fertile, livestock, feedlot, meatpacking, reservation, assembly line,* and *transportation hub.*

- Discuss each term before beginning the activity, using methods described in *Solutions for Effective Instruction.*

- Review each term again with students as it appears in the activity reading and encourage them to use it in their writing.

Writing for Understanding

Phase 1: Gathering Information

1 Prepare for Phase 1 of the activity. Assign students to mixed-ability groups of three and arrange the classroom so students face the screen. If necessary, prepare a transparency that shows students where they will sit. Make one copy each of Information Masters 8A–8C to hand out later to groups at the appropriate tour stop. Also make enough copies of Student Handouts 8B–8D and 8F to give one of each to every student and Student Handout 8G for each group at each of the three corresponding tour stops. For Tour Site 6, each group of six will need 50 copies of the incomplete car image cut from Student Handout 8E. You can precut the images yourself or have students cut them at the site. (**Note:** The "tour" portion of this activity will take about three hour-long periods to complete—one period for Tour Sites 1–3, one period for Tour Sites 4–6, and one period for Tour Sites 7–9. You may want to prepare for only one segment at a time.)

2 Introduce the activity. When students enter the classroom, welcome them to Midwestern Airport. Explain that shortly they will be taking a crop duster tour with their guide, Mr. Ortiz. Ask students to "board their crop dusters." Tell students that on this tour of the Midwest, they will see and learn about nine sites. They will stop at three of the sites to examine visual and written information about the economy, geography, transportation, history, and people of the Midwest region.

3 Play CD Track 28, "Introduction/St. Louis, Missouri: Gateway to the West." This corresponds to the text of Sections 8.1 and 8.2. Have students open their Student Editions and follow along.

4 Pause the CD. As a class, read aloud the question Mr. Ortiz asked. Tell students that they will need to listen for the answer to this question throughout the activity. If desired, write the question on chart paper so students can see it throughout the tour. Then have students turn to Reading Notes 8 in their Interactive Student Notebooks and read the directions. Tell students that they will use the map on this page to draw their route after they visit each site. Each time they fill in the map, ask them to suggest adjectives and key facts about the site. List these suggestions on chart paper and keep them there throughout the tour. (**Note:** Students will use this information to fill in a chart about the Midwest at Step 10.)

Information Masters 8A–8C

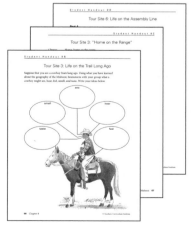

Student Handouts 8B–8G

5 For each site on the tour, project the corresponding transparency and play the corresponding track on the CD. The tour begins with *Transparency 8B: Gateway Arch, St. Louis, Missouri*, and ends with *Transparency 8J: Mall of America, Minnesota*. The text of each CD track corresponds to a section of the Student Edition. Encourage students to read along in their Student Editions. (**Note:** Throughout the activity, pause the CD as often as necessary to ensure student success.)

6 After students visit each site, give them time to work on their Reading Notes. Monitor students' progress.

7 To help students learn about aspects of life in the Midwest over time, have them stop three times to interact with station information and learn about cowboys from long ago, Ford's auto assembly line, and the Mall of America.

- For Tour Site 3, project *Transparency 8D: Dodge City, Kansas, Long Ago* and play CD Track 30, "Dodge City, Kansas: Where the Cattle Once Roamed." When the tour guide indicates that it is time to stop and learn about cowboys from long ago, project a transparency of *Information Master 8A: Tour Site 3: Directions* and pass out a copy to each group. Also, give each student one copy of *Student Handout 8B: Tour Site 3: Life on the Trail Long Ago* and *Student Handout 8C: "Home on the Range."* Have students read and follow the directions for the activity. When students reach Step 3 on Information Master 8A, play CD Track 31, "'Home on the Range' (vocal)." For Step 5 on Information Master 8A, students will stand in a circle to sing their new verses to the song, while you play CD Track 32, "'Home on the Range' (instrumental, with vocal chorus)."

- For Tour Site 6, project *Transparency 8G: Detroit, Michigan: Motor City, USA* and play CD Track 35, "Detroit, Michigan: America's Motor City." When the tour guide indicates that it is time for students to stop and learn more about Ford's assembly line, project a transparency of *Information Master 8B: Tour Site 6: Directions* and pass out a copy to each group. Also, give each student one copy of *Student Handout 8D: Tour Site 6: Life on the Assembly Line*. Have students read and follow the directions for the activity. In Step 3 of Information Master 8B, direct groups of three to create groups of six. Groups will prepare their assembly lines. Each group will need 50 copies of the incomplete Model T image cut from *Student Handout 8E: Tour Site 6: Ford's Model T*. When students are ready, whistle to signal the start of production. After 10 minutes, whistle again to signal the end of production.

- At Tour Site 9, project *Transparency 8J: Mall of America, Minnesota* and play CD Track 38, "Minnesota's Mall of America." When the tour guide indicates that it is time for students to learn more about the Mall of America, project a transparency of *Information Master 8C: Tour Site 9: Directions* and pass out a copy to each group. Also, give each student one copy of *Student Handout 8F: Tour Site 9: Planning a Mall* and one copy of *Student Handout 8G: Tour Site 9: Mall Floor Plan*. Have students read and follow the directions for the activity.

Transparencies 8B–8J

8 **Wrap up the tour.** Have students review and revise their Reading Notes, using pages 118 and 119 of the Student Edition. After the mall maps are completed and posted on the wall, conduct a vote for the mall that students would most like to visit. Then play CD Track 39, "Summary."

Phase 2: Organizing and Synthesizing Information

9 **Prepare for Phase 2 of the activity.** Make enough copies of *Student Handout 8H: Midwest Information Chart* for each student to have one.

10 **Have students categorize key elements of the economy, geography, transportation, history, and people of the Midwest over time.**

- Divide students into groups of four and assign each group one of the following topics related to the Midwest: economy, geography, transportation, history, or people.

- Pass out a copy of Student Handout 8H to each student. Give groups 10 minutes to review the adjectives and the key facts that you recorded on chart paper. Then have groups fill in the appropriate information in their assigned row of the chart.

- When time is up, have each group present the information it included. Tell the other students to record this information on their own charts. Then ask if those students want to add anything to the row, and if it is appropriate, have everyone add it to his or her chart.

11 **Introduce the letter-writing activity.** Tell students that they will write a letter describing their tour of the Midwest. Project a transparency of *Information Master 8D: Writing a Letter About the Midwest* or give one copy to each student. With students, read the directions for writing a letter, clarifying the requirements as needed.

12 **Have students write their letters, and then debrief the activity.** After students have completed their letters, have several volunteers read their letters aloud.

For students who *do not* live in the Midwest, ask:

- What aspects of life in the Midwest did you most enjoy learning about?

- In what ways is life in the Midwest similar to life in your region of the country? In what ways is it different?

- Do you think you would like to live in the Midwest? Why or why not?

- If you were a tour guide like Mr. Ortiz, which one site in the Midwest would you recommend that tourists visit? Explain.

For students who live in the Midwest, ask:

- What aspects of life in the Midwest did you most enjoy learning about?

- Did you learn anything new that surprised you? What was it? Why were you surprised?

Student Handout 8H

Information Master 8D

- Do you like living in the Midwest? Why or why not?

- If you were a tour guide like Mr. Ortiz, which one site in the Midwest would you recommend that tourists visit? Explain.

Reading Further: Detroit During World War II

1 **Project *Transparency 8K: Willow Run Factory*.** Ask the following visual discovery questions to help students analyze the image carefully and make some predictions.

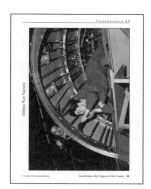

Transparency 8K

- What do you see in this image?

- What do you think these women are doing? *(working to build an airplane)*

- When do you think this photograph was taken? What clues might help you predict the time period? (After students have had a chance to guess, tell them that the photograph was taken in a factory in Detroit, Michigan, during World War II. Many women worked in factories during World War II, helping build things, like airplanes, that were needed for the war.)

- Where were many men during this time? *(away from home, fighting the war)*

- When the United States entered World War II in 1941, many things changed at home. Can you guess what some of those changes might have been in the Midwest?

2 **Have students read Reading Further 8 in the Student Edition.** Allow them to read independently or in small groups.

3 **Have students open their Interactive Student Notebooks to Reading Further 8 and write about Detroit in 1943 from one of two points of view.**

Assessment

Masters for the chapter assessment appear in the *Lesson Masters*. Answers appear below.

Big Ideas

1. B	4. C	7. C
2. C	5. A	8. D
3. D	6. A	

Social Studies Skills

9. A	11. C
10. D	12. B

Show You Know

13. Use four of the bulleted vocabulary terms and one of the bulleted settings as a five-point rubric for this item.

English Language Learners

Before the Geography Challenge activity, create a sentence bank with the correct answers. Have students use this sentence bank to help them complete the Geography Challenge 8 pages in their Interactive Student Notebooks. The sentence bank will enable them to focus on developing their geographic vocabulary and be successful at the same time.

Students with Special Needs

For the Writing for Understanding activity, allow students to create a postcard instead of a letter. Give each student a blank note card and have them decorate one side with pictures from one or more of the sites they visited. Students can then write one or two sentences about their visit to the Midwest, perhaps focusing on just one site and incorporating two or three of the vocabulary words.

Enrichment

Have students research what life was like in a town or city (other than Detroit) in their state during World War II. They can then compare what they discover with what they have learned about Detroit in this chapter. Have students create posters showcasing what they learn about industry, home life, and opportunities in their state during World War II. Allow them to present their posters and findings to the class or to other grades at a school assembly.

Enrichment Resources

LearnTCI

Have students find out more about the Midwest region by exploring the following Enrichment Resources for *Social Studies Alive! Regions of Our Country*, at www.learntci.com.

Internet Connections These recommended Web sites provide useful and engaging content that enforces skills development and mastery of subjects within the chapter.

Enrichment Readings These in-depth readings encourage students to explore selected topics related to the chapter. You may also find readings that relate the chapter's content directly to your state's curriculum.

TeachTCI

For the teachers' resources listed below, click on Enrichment Resources for *Social Studies Alive! Regions of Our Country* at www.teachtci.com.

Biography Bank Hundreds of short biographies of notable people in history are available in PDF format for you to share with your students.

***Study Your State* Resources** Teaching directions and student activity pages (PDF format) will help you guide your students through researching their state.

Additional Reading Opportunities

The following fiction and nonfiction books offer opportunities to extend the content in this chapter.

Great Chicago Fire of 1871 by Kay Melchisedech (Mankato, MN: Capstone, 2006)
This account of the Chicago fire is presented in graphic-novel style, complete with exciting color illustrations, motivating text, and additional resources such as a glossary and Web site listings.

Great Cities of the World: Chicago by Marc Tyler Nobleman (Milwaukee: World Almanac, 2005)
Students will learn about Chicago's history, its job opportunities and recreational activities, and its future. A timeline, maps, and photographs are included.

Henry Ford by Jeffrey Zuehlke (Minneapolis: Lerner, 2007)
This biography of Henry Ford relates how a farm boy from Dearborn, Michigan, became the man who revolutionized manufacturing by introducing the assembly line to American industry.

V Is for Victory: America Remembers World War II by Kathleen Krull (New York: Knopf, 2002)

This "scrapbook" about the homefront during World War II contains copies of primary sources such as ration tickets, posters, photographs, postcards, and headlines. In addition, the informative text provides students with a good grasp of what life was like in the United States during World War II.

Willow Run by Patricia Reilly Giff (New York: Yearling, 2007)

During World War II, Meggie's family moves to Willow Run so her father can work in the factory that manufactures B-24 bombers. This historical fiction tells how war affects families on the homefront.

Use the spaces below to answer the questions on the Geography Challenge Cards. Write complete sentences. On the map, draw and label the feature that answers each question. Exchange your question with another pair of students until you have completed all the cards.

Question 1.   The 12 states in the Midwest are North Dakota, South Dakota, Nebraska, Kansas, Minnesota, Iowa, Missouri, Wisconsin, Illinois, Michigan, Indiana, and Ohio.

Question 2.   The 12 Midwest capital cities are Bismarck, Pierre, Lincoln, Topeka, St. Paul, Des Moines, Jefferson City, Madison, Springfield, Lansing, Indianapolis, and Columbus.

Question 3.   The Great Lakes in the Midwest are Lake Superior, Lake Michigan, Lake Huron, and Lake Erie.

Question 4.   The Black Hills are in South Dakota.

Question 5.   The Mississippi and Missouri rivers come together in St. Louis.

Question 6.   The Ohio River forms part of the borders of Ohio, Indiana, and Illinois.

Question 7.   Michigan, Indiana, Illinois, and Wisconsin border Lake Michigan.

Question 8. Three points of interest in the Midwest are (Gateway Arch, Soo Locks, Mall of America, Mount Rushmore, Crazy Hourse Memorial, O'Hare Airport, Wrigley Field, Dodge City, Detroit).

Question 9. Canada borders the United States to the north of the Midwest region.

Question 10. The main dairy states in the Midwest are Minnesota, Wisconsin, and Michigan.

Your class is taking a tour of the Midwest region. The tour will take you to nine locations. As you move from site to site, draw a line on the map to show your route. After visiting each site, draw a symbol or an image at each location to show what you learned there.

Students' symbols and images for each site will vary.

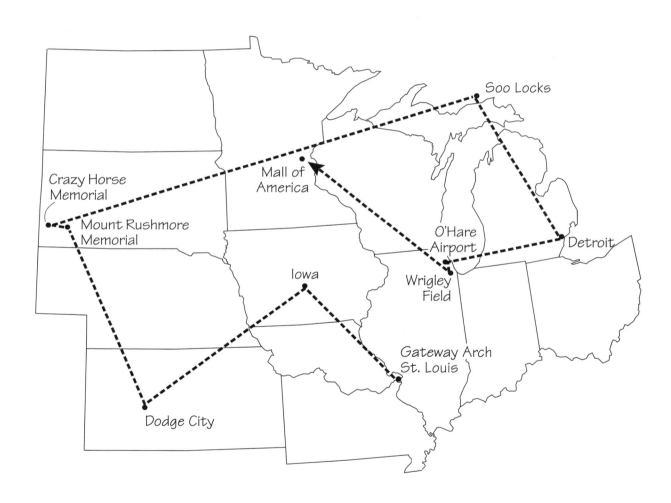

Agricultural Changes in the Midwest

How has farming changed in the Midwest over time?

Overview

Students learn how agriculture in the Midwest changed from 1800 to today. In the Preview, students make and check predictions about farmer productivity over time, and hypothesize explanations. In a Visual Discovery activity, students analyze images of farm life in 1800, 1900, and today. Then they create act-it-outs to demonstrate their understanding of farm life during these periods. In Reading Further, students learn about the importance of the largest crop of the Midwest—corn. In a Processing assignment, they create images of Midwest farming over time.

Objectives

Social Studies

- Graph numerical information from text.
- Make and check predictions, and hypothesize explanations.
- Analyze images.
- Compare and contrast farm size, farm technologies, and farm life from 1800 to today.

Language Arts

- Articulate and support ideas in presentations. (speaking)
- Synthesize information for interview responses. (listening and speaking)

Social Studies Vocabulary

self-sufficient, dairy, reaper, combine, sod, canning, agribusiness, fertilizer, pesticide, maize, renewable resource

Materials

Social Studies Alive! Regions of Our Country

Transparencies 9A–9E

Placards 9A–9I

Interactive Student Notebooks

Lesson Masters

- Student Handouts 9A–9C
- Information Masters 9A–9D

Time Estimates

Preview: 40 min.

Visual Discovery Activity: 3 sessions (60 min. each)

Reading Further: 30 min.

Processing: 30 min.

Activity	Suggested Time	Materials
Preview • Connecting to Prior Knowledge • Building Background Knowledge • Developing Vocabulary	40 minutes	• Interactive Student Notebooks • Preview 9 (1 transparency, made from the Interactive Student Notebook page)
Visual Discovery Exploring Midwest farming across the centuries	*Phase 1* 60 minutes • Farming in 1800 (Steps 1–6)	• *Social Studies Alive! Regions of Our Country,* Sections 9.1–9.4 • Transparencies 9A and 9B • Interactive Student Notebooks • Information Master 9A (1 to 3 copies depending on class size, cut apart)
	Phase 2 60 minutes • Farming in 1900 (Steps 7–12)	• *Social Studies Alive! Regions of Our Country,* Sections 9.5–9.7 • Transparency 9C • Placards 9A–9I • Interactive Student Notebooks • Student Handout 9A (1 copy, cut apart) • Information Master 9B
	Phase 3 60 minutes • Farming today (Steps 13–20)	• *Social Studies Alive! Regions of Our Country,* Sections 9.8–9.10, Summary • Transparency 9D • Interactive Student Notebooks • Student Handout 9B (1 per student) • Student Handout 9C (1 name tag per student, cut apart) • Information Masters 9C and 9D
Reading Further Exploring the many uses of corn	30 minutes	• *Social Studies Alive! Regions of Our Country,* Chapter 9 Reading Further • Transparency 9E • Interactive Student Notebooks
Processing Drawing images of Midwest farming over time	30 minutes	• Interactive Student Notebooks
Assessment	30 minutes	• Chapter 9 Assessment, Lesson Masters • Chapter 9 Assessment, Digital Teacher Resources

Preview

1 **Connecting to Prior Knowledge:** Ask students to think about the foods they ate for breakfast today.

- As students respond, create a list of foods on the board. It is acceptable for students to use a mix of names and types of food (for example, cornflakes, milk, toast, and so on).

- As students look at the list, discuss the following questions: *Which of these foods were made from plants, such as corn or wheat? Which were made from animals? Which are milk products? Where do you think the crops for these foods were grown? Where do you think the animals from which these foods are made were raised? What do you know about farms? What do you think farms are like today?* (**Note:** If your students are very familiar with farms and farming, skip this question.) *How might farms today be similar to or different from farms long ago?*

2 **Building Background Knowledge:** Have students make and check predictions about farmer productivity in the United States.

- Have students open their Interactive Student Notebooks to Preview 9. Introduce the farmer-productivity bar graph. Have students use a sheet of paper to cover the text below the bar graph (Steps 3 and 4).

- At Step 1, project a transparency of Preview 9. Cover Steps 3 and 4, and model for students how to record the information on farmer productivity for 1870, 1920, and 1950. Have students use a crayon to fill in their graphs.

- At Step 2, direct students to use a pencil and predict on their graph the number of people they think were fed by one farmer in 1960 and in 1970.

- At Step 3, ask students to uncover the information below the graph. Tell them to use a crayon to indicate on the graph what really happened to farmer productivity in 1960 and in 1970.

- At Step 4, have students speculate about the causes for the continued increase in farmer productivity by completing the statement at the bottom of the page. Discuss students' responses. Then tell students that in this chapter, they will learn why farmers produce much more food today than they did in the past. Students will discover how farming has changed in the United States over the last 200 years.

3 **Developing Vocabulary:** Introduce key social studies terms—*self-sufficient, dairy, reaper, combine, sod, canning, agribusiness, fertilizer, pesticide, maize,* and *renewable resource.*

- Discuss each term before beginning the activity, using methods described in *Solutions for Effective Instruction.*

- Review each term again with students as it appears in the activity reading and encourage them to use it in their writing.

> ### Vocabulary Development: Illustrate Explanations
>
> Create a two-column class chart, with columns labeled "Word" and "Illustration." As students read the chapter, if they come across social studies terms that relate to farming, have them raise a hand and tell you the word. Write each word in the first column. Then, in the second column, have a volunteer draw an illustration that explains the word's meaning.

Visual Discovery

Phase 1: Farming in 1800

1 Prepare for Phase 1 of the activity. Before class, make enough copies of *Information Master 9A: Midwest Farm Items* to give one item to each student. Cut apart the items and place them in a container.

2 Introduce the activity.

- Project *Transparency 9A: Midwest Farming Over Time*. Tell students that in this chapter, they will explore farming in the Midwest in 1800, 1900, and today. Ask them to identify the appropriate date for each farming image.

- Have students read Section 9.1 in *Social Studies Alive! Regions of Our Country*.

- Focus students' attention on the graphic organizer in Section 9.1. Ask these questions: *What kind of equipment is pictured here?* (a plow from 1800, a plow from 1900, a modern tractor) *What do you think this equipment is used for?* (plowing fields to prepare them for planting) *How has farm equipment changed over the last 200 years? How might improvements in farm equipment have made the farmer's job easier? What other changes might have happened in farming over time?*

3 Have students analyze an image of Midwest farming in 1800. Project *Transparency 9B: Midwest Farming in 1800*. Ask these questions: *What does this picture show? What structures can you identify? What tools do you see? What birds and animals can you identify? What are the people doing?*

4 Have students learn about Midwest farming in 1800. Ask them to read Sections 9.2–9.4 in their Student Editions.

5 Have students give presentations on the significance of different farm items in 1800.

- Begin by having each student draw a farm item from the container and read it silently.

- Ask students to look at Transparency 9B again. Have them find their item and its corresponding number in the picture.

- Explain that each student will stand in front of the transparency, point to his or her item, identify what it is, and describe why it was important to farm families in 1800. Model this procedure. Tell students that you have been assigned Farm Item 11. Say: *This is a pitchfork. This was important because it helped the farmer harvest hay and feed the animals.*

- Divide the class into two groups. Students from one group should line up in numerical order at the side of the image. The second group is the audience. Ask each student to move in front of the image, make his or her presentation, and then sit down. When the first group is finished, have these students become the audience, while the members of the second group make their presentations.

Information Master 9A

Transparencies 9A and 9B

> **Reading Strategy: Anticipate Content**
>
> Before students begin reading, ask them to respond to these true/false statements: Farming has been important in the Midwest for centuries. (T or F) Farming tools and practices have changed little since the 1800s. (T or F) Once students have responded to the statements, ask them to read the text. Then have them reconsider the statements in light of the new information they have learned.

6 **Have students graph information from the text about farming in 1800.** Have students open their Interactive Student Notebooks to the first two pages of Reading Notes 9. You may want to allow students to work in pairs to complete the pages.

Phase 2: Farming in 1900

7 **Prepare for Phase 2 of the activity.** Cut apart the descriptions on *Student Handout 9A: Preparing for Act-It-Outs.* Familiarize yourself with *Information Master 9B: Sample Interview 1,* which you will use to model the activity for students.

8 **Have students analyze an image of Midwest farming in 1900.** Project *Transparency 9C: Midwest Farming in 1900.* Ask these questions: *What does this picture show? What buildings, structures, and tools can you identify? Looking at this picture, do you think farm life in 1900 was easier than, more difficult than, or the same as farm life in 1800? Why do you think that?*

9 **Have students learn about Midwest farming in 1900.** Ask them to read Sections 9.5–9.7 in their Student Editions.

Information Master 9B

10 **Direct students to prepare for interview act-it-outs about farming in 1900.**

- Assign students to mixed-ability groups of four.

- Tell students that they will "step into the shoes" of one person who might have lived and worked on a farm in the 1900s. Assign each group the role of one of the following characters: farmer, farmwife, older daughter, younger daughter, older son, younger son, hired hand 1, or hired hand 2.

- Distribute *Placards 9A–9H: Farm Characters in 1900* and the corresponding directions cut from Student Handout 9A to the appropriate groups. (**Note:** Keep *Placard 9I: Woman Washing Clothes on Midwest Farm in 1900* and the corresponding directions to model the activity).

- Explain that groups will have five minutes to follow the guidelines they have been given to prepare for an interview about their characters' lives. Review the directions with them.

- Model the activity with two volunteers. Ask the class to look at Transparency 9C again. Have one volunteer hold up Placard 9I. Have the other volunteer be the interviewer. As you stand beside the placard holder, pantomime washing clothes on a washboard. At the same time, have the interviewer ask you the questions for this character that appear on Student Handout 9A.

- Give groups 5 to 10 minutes to prepare for the act-it-outs.

11 **Have students perform interview act-it-outs about farming in 1900.**

- Choose two students from each group to participate in the act-it-out. One will display the placard; the other will assume the character's role. Have students arrange themselves appropriately in front of the projected image.

Transparency 9C

Placards 9A–9I

- Tell the class that you are going to interview the people living and working on this farm. During the act-it-out, assume the role of an on-scene reporter and interview the characters, asking the questions that the students have discussed in their groups.

12 Have students graph information from the text about farming in 1900. Ask students to complete the third and fourth pages of Reading Notes 9 in their Interactive Student Notebooks. You may want to allow students to work in pairs. Ask them to look at the graphs on the left-hand page. Make it clear to students that, before they fill in the second column of each bar graph, they need to copy the information from the bar graphs on the first page of Reading Notes 9.

Phase 3: Farming Today

13 Prepare for Phase 3 of the activity. Make enough copies of *Student Handout 9B: Newspaper Article* to give one to each student. Also, make enough copies of *Student Handout 9C: Name Tags* so that you can give one tag to each student, and cut apart the name tags. Familiarize yourself with *Information Master 9C: Sample Interview 2,* which you will use to model the activity for students.

14 Have students analyze an image of Midwest farming today. Project *Transparency 9D: Midwest Farming Today.* Tell students that the people in this image have gathered for a farm auction. If necessary, briefly describe what an auction is. Then ask these questions: *What do you see? How has farm equipment changed since 1900? Do you think this new equipment has changed farm life? How else might farm life be different today? How might farm life be the same?*

15 Have students learn about farming today. Ask them to read Sections 9.8–9.10 and the Summary in their Student Editions.

16 Direct students to prepare for interview act-it-outs about a farm auction today.

- Divide the class into mixed-ability groups of four.

- Give a copy of Student Handout 9B to each student. Have the class read the article.

- Assign one of the following roles to each group: farm family member, banker, local business owner, or neighbor. Distribute the appropriate name tags cut from Student Handout 9C, one for each group member. Have students use tape to attach their name tags.

- Project a transparency of *Information Master 9D: Directions for the Auction Act-It-Out* and review the directions.

- Model the activity. Ask a volunteer to join you. Ask him or her to act as the reporter and ask the questions on Information Master 9D. Pretend that you are a local business owner. Answer the questions the reporter asks you.

Student Handouts 9B and 9C

Information Masters 9C and 9D

Transparency 9D

17 Have students perform interview act-it-outs about a farm auction today.

- When groups are ready, select one member from each group to participate in the act-it-out. During the act-it-out, interview the characters, asking questions similar to those they discussed in their groups. (**Option:** Model the job of reporter, and then have students take turns acting as the reporter.)

- If time permits, repeat the act-it-outs until all students have had a chance to be interviewed and/or have had a turn as the reporter.

18 Have the entire class interact at the auction. Tell students that now they will all "attend" the auction. They should circulate around the room and talk to people from other groups. As they meet with other students, they should express how they feel about the auction and how the auction affects them.

19 Have students graph information from the text about farming today. Ask students to complete the last two pages of Reading Notes 9 in their Interactive Student Notebooks. You may want to allow students to work in pairs. Have them look at the graphs on the left-hand page. Make it clear to students that they are to copy information from the bar graphs on the third page of the Reading Notes before they fill out the last column.

20 Debrief the activity.

- Have students look at their completed graphs on the left-hand page. Ask the following questions:

- What happened over time to the number of Americans living on farms? *(The number of people living on farms decreased over time.)*

- What happened to the number of acres of the average farm over time? *(The number of acres per farm increased.)*

- What does that mean? *(That means that it now takes fewer people to farm more land than it did in the past.)*

- What does that tell us about farmer productivity? *(If fewer farmers can feed more people today than they could in the past, that means farmer productivity has increased.)*

- Why might that be true? (**Hint:** Think about the changes in farm equipment from 1800 to today.)

Ask students to turn back a few pages to Step 4 of Preview 9 and look at their hypotheses about the reasons for increased farmer productivity. Ask:

- Did you guess correctly about why one farmer fed more people over time?

- If you guessed incorrectly, how would you finish that sentence now?

Reading Strategy: Anticipate Content

Before students read Sections 9.8–9.10, have them respond to these true/false statements: It takes longer today to raise a bushel of wheat than it did in the 1800s. (T or F) The most important new farm tool of the last 100 years is the tractor. (T or F) More and more people start farms today than ever before. (T or F) Once students have responded to the statements, have them read the text. Then, with the new information they have learned, students may revisit and reconsider the statements.

Reading Further: Corn: Key Crop of the Midwest

1 **Project *Transparency 9E: Corn Palace Mural, Mitchell, South Dakota*.**
Ask the following visual discovery questions to help students analyze the
image carefully and make some predictions.

- What do you see? Describe it in as much detail as you can.

- What might this be? (Students may guess that it is a painting. After they
  have had a chance to respond fully, tell them that it is a mural made of
  corn cobs.)

- Are you surprised to learn that this is made from corn? Why or why not?

- What might be important about this mural? Why might people use corn
  in this way?

2 **Have students read Reading Further 9 in their Student Editions.** Allow
them to read independently or in small groups.

3 **Have students think about some possible uses of corn in the future.** Ask
students to open their Interactive Student Notebooks to Reading Further 9.
Review the directions. Have students complete the page. If time permits, have
them share their writing with the class.

Transparency 9E

Processing

1 **Have students open their Interactive Student Notebooks to Processing 9 to
draw items that represent farming at different times.** Review the directions
with students. Have them complete the page. If time permits, students can
share their pictures with partners.

Assessment

Masters for the chapter assessment appear in the *Lesson Masters*. Answers
appear below.

Big Ideas

1. A	5. C	9. A
2. D	6. C	10. B
3. C	7. D	
4. B	8. D	

Social Studies Skills

11. 1800

12. reaper

13. cow

Show You Know

14. The three bulleted points and the drawing can serve as a four-point rubric
for this item.

English Language Learners

Make copies of Transparencies 9B–9D, which show images of farms in 1800, 1900, and today. Before the Visual Discovery activity, have students label items in the pictures. This will help them become familiar with the vocabulary associated with farming. It will also provide students with an additional reference during the activity.

Students with Special Needs

During the presentations in Phase 1 of the activity, allow students to use the farm item modeled by the teacher. This will enable them to participate in the presentations without the additional burden of figuring out the item's use. During the act-it-outs in Phase 2 of the activity, allow students to hold a placard. During Phase 3 of the activity, when the entire class mingles at the farm auction, have students walk around the classroom with a partner. This will allow them to participate without having to answer questions by themselves.

Enrichment

Have students collect examples of different uses of corn, such as labels from food products or advertisements for cars that use ethanol. Then have students create a mural from their collected items, showing the many uses of corn in the United States.

Enrichment Resources

LearnTCI

Have students find out more about the history of farming in the Midwest region by exploring the following Enrichment Resources for *Social Studies Alive! Regions of Our Country,* at www.learntci.com.

Internet Connections These recommended Web sites provide useful and engaging content that enforces skills development and mastery of subjects within the chapter.

Enrichment Readings These in-depth readings encourage students to explore selected topics related to the chapter. You may also find readings that relate the chapter's content directly to your state's curriculum.

TeachTCI

For the teachers' resources listed below, click on Enrichment Resources for *Social Studies Alive! Regions of Our Country* at www.teachtci.com.

Biography Bank Hundreds of short biographies of notable people in history are available in PDF format for you to share with your students.

***Study Your State* Resources** Teaching directions and student activity pages (PDF format) will help you guide your students through researching their state.

Additional Reading Opportunities

The following books offer opportunities to extend the content in this chapter.

Dust to Eat by Michael L. Cooper (New York: Clarion Books, 2001)
This book tells the story of the Dust Bowl in the 1930s. Photographs from the period help students understand the hardships and challenges that Midwesterners faced during that time.

Farmland Innovator: A Story about Cyrus McCormick by Catherine A. Welch (Minneapolis: Lerner, 2007)
This book tells the story of how the McCormick reaper revolutionized wheat farming in the Midwest.

A Pioneer Farm Girl: The Diary of Sarah Gillespie 1877–1878 by Suzanne L. Bunkers (Mankato, MN: Capstone, 2000)
Students learn about the hardships and dangers that settlers had to face while making the journey to the Great Plains. Activities help students make real-world connections to this time period.

Pioneers of the Frontier by Charles Sundling (Edina, MN: Abdo, 2000)
Maps and color photographs help students learn about what the pioneers were like and how they turned the Great Plains into America's breadbasket.

9.2 Below are the beginnings of two bar graphs. Color boxes in the first graph red to show the number of Americans, out of 100, who lived on a farm in 1800. Color boxes in the second graph blue to show the average size of a farm in 1800.

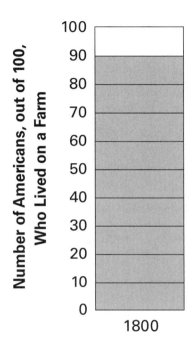

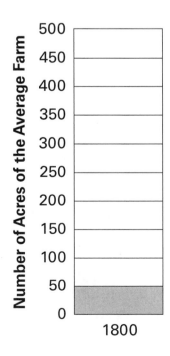

9.3 In the boxes below, draw two tools that farmers used in 1800.

Drawings will vary.

Drawings will vary.

9.4 Write one sentence in each thought bubble to tell about farm life in 1800.

Answers will vary.

Answers will vary.

Answers will vary.

9.5 Continue filling in the bar graphs. Copy information from page 54 in the first column of each graph. Then complete the second column of each graph. Color the appropriate number of spaces on the first graph red. Color the appropriate number of spaces on the second graph blue.

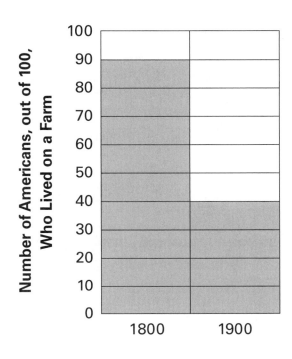

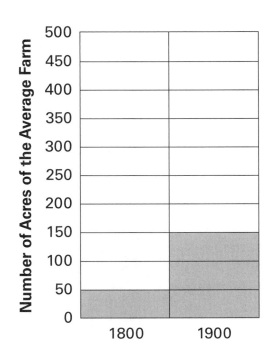

9.6 In the boxes below, draw two tools that farmers used in 1900.

Drawings will vary.

Drawings will vary.

9.7 Write one sentence in each thought bubble to tell about farm life in 1900.

Answers will vary.

Answers will vary.

Answers will vary.

9.8 Complete the bar graphs. Copy information from page 56 in the first two columns of each graph. Then complete the third column of each graph. Color the appropriate number of spaces on the first graph red. Color the appropriate number of spaces on the second graph blue.

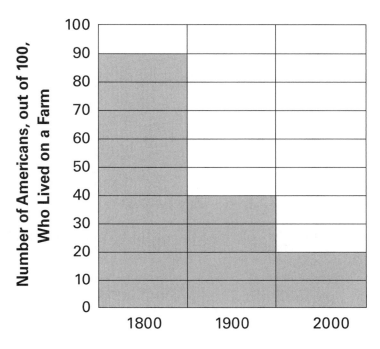

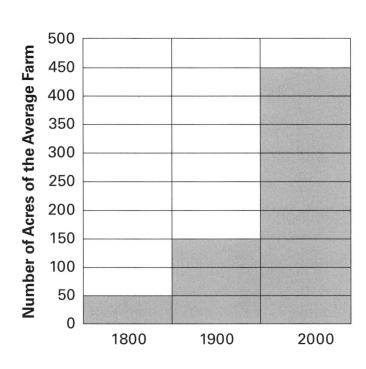

9.9 In the boxes below, draw two tools that farmers used in 2000.

Drawings will vary.	Drawings will vary.

9.10 Write one sentence in each thought bubble to tell about farm life in 2000.

Answers will vary.

Answers will vary.

Answers will vary.

A Big Rig Tour of the Southwest

How have geography and history shaped life in the Southwest?

Overview

In this lesson, students take a "big rig tour" of the Southwest region of the United States. In the Preview activity, a Geography Challenge introduces students to the Southwest. In a Writing for Understanding activity, groups of three students sit in big rigs, listen to a tour guide, and view nine images of places in the Southwest. The trucks stop at three sites, where students learn key concepts and facts about the region through interactive experiences. In a Reading Further activity, students act as newspaper reporters writing about the Battle of the Alamo. The writing activity serves as the Processing assignment for the chapter.

Objectives

Social Studies
- Trace the path of a tour through the Southwest on a map of the region.
- Analyze the design of the Hoover Dam.
- Identify the challenges faced by people along the U.S.-Mexico border.
- Reenact and describe the land rush in Oklahoma.

Language Arts
- Gather information from an audio tour. (listening)
- Synthesize information into letter form. (writing)
- Write a newspaper article. (writing)

Social Studies Vocabulary

mesa, desert, adapt, aqueduct, dam, canyon, cave, cavern, border, mission, rebellion, capital

Materials

Social Studies Alive! Regions of Our Country

Transparencies 10A–10K

Interactive Student Notebooks

Lesson Masters
- Student Handouts 10A–10H
- Information Masters 10A–10D

CD 2, Tracks 1–10

Interactive Desk Map or large U.S. map

Time Estimates

Preview: 45 min.

Writing for Understanding: 4 sessions (varying lengths)

Reading Further: 35 min.

Activity	Suggested Time	Materials
Preview • Connecting to Prior Knowledge • Building Background Knowledge: Geography Challenge • Developing Vocabulary	45 minutes	• *Social Studies Alive! Regions of Our Country,* Section 10.1 • Transparency 10A • Interactive Student Notebooks • Student Handout 10A (depending on class size, 1 or 2 copies, cut apart) • Interactive Desk Map or large U.S. map
Writing for Understanding Writing a letter synthesizing information about the Southwest	*Phase 1* 60-minute sessions (3) • Introduction and Tour Sites 1–3 • Tour Sites 4–6 • Tour Sites 7–9 (Steps 1–9) *Phase 2* 45-minute session • Letter writing (Steps 10 and 11)	• *Social Studies Alive! Regions of Our Country,* Sections 10.1–10.10 and Summary • Transparencies 10B–10J • Interactive Student Notebooks • Information Masters 10A–10C (1 copy per group of 3, plus 1 transparency) • Student Handouts 10B and 10D (1 copy of each per group of 3) • CD 2, Tracks 1–10 • Information Master 10D (1 per student or 1 transparency) • Student Handout 10C and 10F (2-4 copies, depending on class size) • Student Handout 10E and 10H (1 copy of each per student) • Student Handout 10G (7 copies of first page, 4 copies of second page)
Reading Further Writing a newspaper article	35 minutes	• *Social Studies Alive! Regions of Our Country,* Chapter 10 Reading Further • Transparency 10K • Interactive Student Notebooks
Processing The letter-writing assignment serves as the Processing activity for this chapter.		
Assessment	30 minutes	• Chapter 10 Assessment, Lesson Masters • Chapter 10 Assessment, Digital Teacher Resources

Preview

1 **Preparing for the Preview:** Before class, cut out the questions from *Student Handout 10A: Geography Challenge Cards.* (**Note:** You may want to laminate the cards for future use.)

2 **Connecting to Prior Knowledge:** Introduce students to the Southwest region.

Student Handout 10A

- Tell students that the next region of the United States they will be learning about is the Southwest. To help students see where the Southwest region lies within the country, hold up the Interactive Desk Map or display a large map of the United States and point out the region.

- Have students examine the graphic organizer in Section 10.1 of *Social Studies Alive! Regions of Our Country.* Ask: *What states do you see on this map of the Southwest? What would you like to learn about this region?* Tell students that they will be taking a tour of important places in the Southwest. Explain that the dots on the map show the locations of places they will visit on the tour.

- Project *Transparency 10A: The Southwest Region.* Explain that all the places shown in the collage are in the Southwest.

Transparency 10A

- Ask students to examine the collage of Southwest images and then answer the questions on Preview 10 in their Interactive Student Notebooks. Discuss their responses and tell them that in this chapter, they will map features of the Southwest as they take a big rig tour around the region with their tour guide, Mr. Nakai.

3 **Building Background Knowledge: Geography Challenge**

- Assign students to mixed-ability pairs. Pass out one Geography Challenge question to each pair.

- Have students open their Student Editions to pages 152 and 153 and their Interactive Student Notebooks to Geography Challenge 10. Review the directions with students and model completing one question before pairs work independently.

- Monitor students' work, using Guide to Geography Challenge 10, found at the end of the lesson. After a pair finishes a card, have both students raise their hands to indicate that they are ready for you to check their work. When necessary, instruct students to revise their answers. Remind pairs to exchange cards with other pairs until all pairs have completed most or all of the questions. Alternately, you may want to create a "Card Bank" pile on a desk in the classroom, from which students can obtain new questions.

- Review with students the correct answers to the Geography Challenge. As you discuss the answers, students should again look at the maps of the Southwest region on pages 152 and 153 of the Student Edition.

4 **Developing Vocabulary:** Introduce key social studies terms—*mesa, desert, adapt, aqueduct, dam, canyon, cave, cavern, border, mission, rebellion,* and *capital.*

- Discuss each term before beginning the activity, using methods described in *Solutions for Effective Instruction.*

- Review each term again with students as it appears in the activity reading, and encourage them to use it in their writing.

Writing for Understanding

Phase 1: Gathering Information

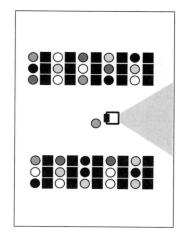

1 **Prepare for Phase 1 of the activity.** Assign students to mixed-ability groups of three and arrange the classroom according to the diagram. If necessary, prepare a transparency that shows students where they will sit. Make copies of Information Masters and Student Handouts to give to students and groups at appropriate stops on the tour.

- For Tour Site 3, make one copy of Student Handout 10B for each group. Make a transparency of Information Master 10A and a copy for each group.

- For Tour Site 6, make one copy each per group of Information Master 10B and Student Handout 10D, and one copy of Student Handout 10E for each student. Make two to three copies of Student Handout 10C and cut out one role card for every three students.

- For Tour Site 9, prepare a large area, such as a cafeteria, gymnasium, or playing field, for the Oklahoma settlement activity. You may want to place string or masking tape on the floor or ground to designate the borders of Oklahoma. Make a transparency of Information Master 10C and a copy of each transparency for each group. Make enough copies of Student Handout 10F so that each student will have one card. Cut the cards apart. Make seven copies of the first page of Student Handout 10G and four copies of the second page; then cut out the Fate Cards. You might want to copy these onto card stock to make them sturdy for students to handle. Make one copy of Student Handout 10H for each student.

(**Note:** The "tour" portion of this activity will take about three hour-long class periods to complete, one period for Tour Sites 1–3, one period for Tour Sites 4–6, and one period for Tour Sites 7–9. You may want to prepare for only one tour segment at a time.)

2 **Introduce the activity.** Welcome students to the Southwestern Trucking Terminal as they enter the classroom. Explain that they will take a big rig tour with their guide, Mr. Nakai. Project the seating chart and ask students to "board their big rigs." Tell students that on this tour of the Southwest, they will see and learn about nine sites. The big rigs will stop at three of the sites for students to examine visual and written information about the history, economy, government, geography, and people of the Southwest region.

3 **Play the first part of CD 2, Track 1, "Introduction/Monument Valley: Home of the Navajos."** This corresponds to the text of Section 10.1 in the Student Edition. Have students open their books and follow along.

4 **Pause the CD.** Have students turn to Reading Notes 10 in their Interactive Student Notebooks and read the directions. Tell students that they will use the map on this page to draw their route after they visit each site. Have them draw symbols on their maps to show what they learned at each place. As an extension, ask volunteers to describe each site with adjectives and key facts about the place.

5 **For each site on the tour, project the corresponding transparency and play the corresponding track on the CD.** The tour begins with *Transparency 10B: Monument Valley* and ends with *Transparency 10J: Guthrie, Oklahoma, Land Rush.* The text of each CD track corresponds to a section of the Student Edition. Encourage students to read along in their Student Editions. To begin the tour, play the remainder of CD 2, Track 1. (**Note:** Throughout the activity, pause the CD as often as necessary to ensure student success.)

6 **After students visit each site, give them time to work on their Reading Notes.** Monitor students' progress.

7 **To allow students to analyze the design of the Hoover Dam, identify the challenges faced by people along the U.S.-Mexico border, and reenact and describe a land rush in Oklahoma, have them get out of their big rigs three times.**

- For Tour Site 3, project *Transparency 10D: Hoover Dam* and play CD 2, Track 3, "Hoover Dam: A Concrete Marvel." When the tour guide indicates that students should get off the big rigs, pause the CD. Pass out a copy of *Student Handout 10B: Tour Site 3: Learning About the Building of Hoover Dam* to each group. Read the activity directions with the class. Give each group poster board or butcher paper, and crayons or colored markers. Have groups work on their solutions for Problem 1. When groups are ready, have each present their proposal for Problem 1 and then listen carefully to the other groups' proposals. Conduct a class vote on the proposal they think is best. Repeat this process for Problems 2 and 3. Then project a transparency of *Information Master 10A: Tour Site 3: Solutions Used in the Building of Hoover Dam* and pass out a copy of it to each group. Have volunteers read aloud the solutions that were chosen by Hoover Dam engineers.

- For Tour Site 6, project *Transparency 10G: U.S.-Mexico Border* and play CD 2, Track 6, "El Paso and Ciudad Juárez: Two Cities, Two Countries, One Border." Pass out a copy of *Information Master 10B: Tour Site 6: Learning About the U.S.–Mexico Border near El Paso, Texas* to each group. Also distribute one role card from *Student Handout 10C: Act-It-Out Role Cards* and one copy of *Student Handout 10D: Tour Site 6: Learning About the U.S.–Mexico Border near El Paso, Texas.* Have students read and follow the directions for the activity. When it is time, have all students who prepared to role-play Mexican Politicians step to the front of the room.

Transparencies 10B–10J

Student Handouts 10B–10E

Information Masters 10A–10B

Interview them, while the rest of the class acts as the press corps. Repeat the process for the other three roles. Then distribute a copy of *Student Handout 10E: Challenges at the U.S.–Mexico Border* to each student and have them complete the page.

- For Tour Site 9, project a transparency of Information Master 10C and play CD 2, Track 9, "Guthrie, Oklahoma: Center of the Land Rush." Read the directions with students. Pass out one card from *Student Handout 10F: Land Rush Role Cards* to each student. Have students stand side by side along the "border" you have created for Oklahoma. Arrange the cards from *Student Handout 10G: Land Rush Fate Cards* facedown, randomly, within the borders of the state. Tell students that these cards will determine how well they succeed in Oklahoma. Explain that some cards have positive fates; there are only 12 of these in all. Other cards have negative fates. This simulates that less than half of land rush participants were successful in Oklahoma. Have students reenact the settlement of Oklahoma by following the instructions on *Information Master 10C: Tour Site 9: Learning About the Settlement of Oklahoma in Guthrie, Oklahoma.* (**Note:** American Indians were settled most densely in the eastern part of the state; ranchers and boomers were mostly in the western part. You may want to have the students playing these roles stand in the corresponding areas.) Ask the following questions during the activity:

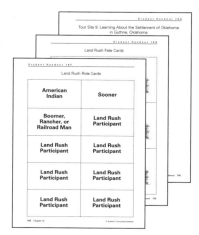

Student Handouts 10F–10H

- When American Indians move into Indian Territory, ask: *How do you feel about being moved to a new home? How do you feel about having your own area, far away from white settlers?*

- When boomers, ranchers, and railroad workers move into Indian Territory, ask: *Why have you decided to move into Indian Territory? This territory was set aside for American Indians. How will you deal with them, since they own this land?*

Information Master 10C

- Just before sooners and land rush participants move into Oklahoma, ask the American Indians: *What do you think about the land rush? How do you think it might change your lives?* Ask the boomers, ranchers, and railroad workers: *What do you think of the land rush? How do you think it might change your lives?*

- After the interviews, distribute copies of *Student Handout 10H: Tour Site 9: About the Settlement of Oklahoma in Guthrie, Oklahoma,* and have students complete the page.

8 **After the tour, give students a few minutes to complete Reading Notes 10.** Then have them check their Reading Notes and Student Handout answers against the Student Edition.

9 **To wrap up the tour, play CD 2, Track 10, "Summary," and have students follow along in the Student Edition.** Hold a brief class discussion about which sites students enjoyed visiting most on the tour.

Vocabulary Development: Illustrate a Dictionary

After listening to CD 2, Track 10, "Summary," have students create an illustrated dictionary of the social studies terms in this chapter. For each entry, students should include a definition, an illustration, and a sentence using the term in their own words.

Phase 2: Synthesizing Information

10 **Project a transparency of *Information Master 10D: Writing a Letter About the Southwest* or distribute one copy to each student.** Read the directions with students, clarifying the requirements. Then have students write their letters.

11 **Debrief the activity.** After students have completed their letters, have several volunteers read their letters aloud. Afterward, discuss these questions:

For students who do *not* live in the Southwest:

- What aspects of life in the Southwest did you most enjoy learning about in this activity?

- In what ways is life in the Southwest similar to life in your region of the country? In what ways is it different?

- Do you think you would like to live in the Southwest? Why or why not?

- If you were a tour guide like Mr. Nakai, which site in the Southwest would you recommend that tourists visit? Explain.

For students who live in the Southwest:

- What aspects of life in the Southwest did you most enjoy learning about?

- Did you learn anything new that surprised you? What was it? Why were you surprised?

- Do you like living in the Southwest? Why or why not?

- If you were a tour guide like Mr. Nakai, which site in the Southwest would you recommend that tourists visit? Explain.

Information Master 10D

> **Writing Tip: Use Descriptive Words**
>
> Before students write their letters, brainstorm descriptive words they might use to describe places they visited on their tour. To encourage "rich" descriptive words, have students consult a thesaurus.

Reading Further: Freedom—or Death

1 **Project *Transparency 10K: Battle of the Alamo.***

- Ask: *What do you think is happening in this painting? What details make you think so?*

- Tell students that the painting shows the Battle of the Alamo, which they read a little about in Section 10.8. Ask: *Can you tell which people in the painting are Texans and which are Mexican soldiers? How can you tell?*

- Tell students that they will read more about the Battle of the Alamo and the impact it had on the Texas Revolution. Explain to students that at the start of the Texas Revolution, the U.S. government did not want to support the Texans against the Mexican army.

2 **Have students read Reading Further 10 in their Student Editions, independently or in small groups.**

3 **After students have finished reading, debrief with the class.** Ask: *What happened at the Battle of the Alamo? Why do you think the Texans were determined to try to win?*

Transparency 10K

4 Have students act as reporters for different newspapers, writing about the recent Battle at the Alamo.

- Have students open their Interactive Student Notebooks to Reading Further 10. Read the directions with students and have them complete the page.

- Assign one-third of the class to be reporters for a San Antonio newspaper, another third of the class to be reporters for a Washington, D.C., newspaper, and the final third of the class to be reporters for a Mexico City, Mexico, newspaper.

- Discuss with the class what a reporter from each place might write about the battle. Brainstorm the different viewpoints people from each place might hold and the important points students might want to include in their articles. Create a list of ideas on the board to aid student writing.

- Have students write their articles for Reading Further 10 in their Interactive Student Notebooks. When they are finished, invite students to share their articles with the class. Discuss how the articles in the three newspapers are similar and different.

- You might want to compile students' articles into three binders, representing the different newspapers.

Assessment

Masters for the chapter assessment appear in the *Lesson Masters*. Answers appear below.

Big Ideas

1. B	5. A	9. C
2. D	6. B	10. A
3. C	7. A	
4. C	8. D	

Social Studies Skills

11. Texas

12. Arizona

13. oil, coal

14. coal

Show You Know

15. The sites, cities, and states can provide a rubric for this item.

English Language Learners

To help students with sentence structure and vocabulary as they write their letters, create a template that they can fill in for the first site they choose to write about. Students can write their own introduction, possibly with the help of a peer. Then have students fill in the template. They can copy the template for the next two sites they choose to write about.

As we visited _____ *, the most interesting*

thing I saw was _____ *. I found*

this interesting because _____

_____ *. The best way to describe*

this is _____

_____ *. I learned about so many things on this visit;*

for example, _____

_____ *.*

Students with Special Needs

For the letter-writing activity, have students focus on only one site they visited. Give students appropriate vocabulary words related to the site they chose for their letter. If students want to focus on more than one site, have them draw pictures of the three sites they visited. Then have students write a short caption for each picture.

Enrichment

Have students compile all the newspaper articles from the Reading Further activity into an actual newspaper. Students could create a newspaper name and add creative headlines, pictures, captions, and even advertisements. If possible, make copies of the newspaper to distribute to the class.

Enrichment Resources

LearnTCI

Have students find out more about the Southwest region by exploring the following Enrichment Resources for *Social Studies Alive! Regions of Our Country,* at www.learntci.com.

Internet Connections These recommended Web sites provide useful and engaging content that enforces skills development and mastery of subjects within the chapter.

Enrichment Readings These in-depth readings encourage students to explore selected topics related to the chapter. You may also find readings that relate the chapter's content directly to your state's curriculum.

TeachTCI

For the teachers' resources listed below, click on Enrichment Resources for *Social Studies Alive! Regions of Our Country* at www.teachtci.com.

Biography Bank Hundreds of short biographies of notable people in history are available in PDF format for you to share with your students.

***Study Your State* Resources** Teaching directions and student activity pages (PDF format) will help you guide your students through researching their state.

Additional Reading Opportunities

The following fiction and nonfiction books offer opportunities to extend the content in this chapter.

Cowboys on the Western Trail: The Cattle Drive Adventures of Joshua McNabb and Davy Bartlett by Eric Oatman (Washington, D.C.: National Geographic, 2004)

This historical fiction helps students understand the challenges, the dangers, and the adventure of a cattle drive. Students travel the trail from southern Texas to Nebraska, with archival photographs, colorful illustrations, a map, and engaging text bringing the journey to life.

The Battle of the Alamo by Matt Doeden. Illustrated by Charles Barnett III and Phil Miller. (Mankato, MN: Capstone, 2005)

This account of the Alamo is presented in comic-book style—exciting colored illustrations and easy-to-read text—with additional resources, including Web site recommendations.

The Navajos by Liz Sonneborn (Minneapolis: Lerner, 2007)

This book presents a history of the Navajos through illustrations, color photographs, and interesting facts about their traditions and current affairs.

Use the spaces below to answer the questions on the Geography Challenge Cards. Write complete sentences. On the map, draw and label the feature that answers each question. Exchange your question with another pair of students until you have completed all the cards.

Question 1. Which four states are in the Southwest region?
The four states in the Southwest region are Arizona, New Mexico, Texas, and Oklahoma.

Question 2. What body of water has oil deposits along its shoreline?
The Gulf of Mexico has oil deposits along its shoreline.

Question 3. What minerals can be found near the "Four Corners" area?
Coal, uranium, and oil or natural gas can be found near the Four Corners area.

Question 4. What are the state capitals in this region?
The state capitals in this region are Phoenix, Arizona; Santa Fe, New Mexico; Austin, Texas; and Oklahoma City, Oklahoma.

Question 5. Which river forms part of the border between the United States and Mexico?
The Rio Grande forms part of the border between the United States and Mexico.

Question 6. What famous site is near Hoover Dam?
The Grand Canyon is a famous site near Hoover Dam.

Question 7. What is the highest point in the Southwest region?
The highest point in the Southwest region is Wheeler Peak.

Question 8. Which river runs through the Grand Canyon and flows into Mexico?

The Colorado River runs through the Grand Canyon and flows into Mexico.

Question 9. What country borders the United States south of New Mexico?

The country of Mexico borders the United States south of New Mexico.

Question 10. Which state in the Southwest is the largest manufacturing state?

Texas is the largest manufacturing state in the Southwest.

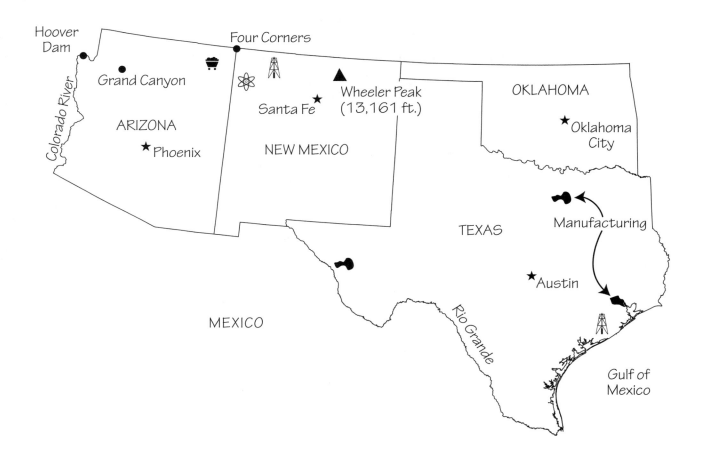

Your class is taking a big rig tour of the Southwest region. The tour will take you to nine locations. As you move from site to site, draw a line on the map to show your route. After visiting each site, draw a symbol or an image at that location to show what you learned there.

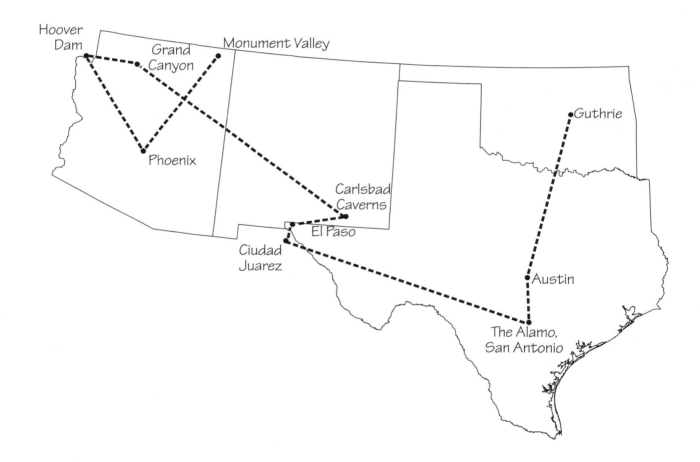

Suppose that you are a newspaper reporter in 1836. You want to write about the Battle of the Alamo that just took place in San Antonio. Answer the questions below. Then use your answers as notes to help you write your article.

Who fought at the Battle of the Alamo?

General Santa Anna's Mexican army fought against Texan soldiers.

Why were they fighting?

Texans were fighting to defend the mission and to gain Texan independence. The Mexican army was fighting to keep Texas part of Mexico.

What details might your readers want to know?

Students' answers will vary depending on which newspaper they are writing for.

A Case Study in Water Use: The Colorado River

How do people depend on the Colorado River and share its water?

Overview

Students explore the history of how people have used and shared the water of the Colorado River. In the Preview, students use a map to explore the geography of the Colorado River Basin. Then, in an Experiential Exercise, students act out the roles of people living near the Colorado River in four different time periods to understand how its water has been used and shared, and how it might be in the future. In Reading Further, students study the impact of floods on the Havasupai tribe and analyze the impact of water on life in Supai, Arizona. During the Processing activity, students create a poster to educate people about the future challenges for water users in the Colorado River Basin.

Objectives

Social Studies

- Identify geographic features in the Colorado River Basin.
- Identify the impact of limited resources on people.
- Enact the experiences of groups that have shared water from the Colorado River.
- Make predictions about water resources.
- Create a map of water users along the Colorado River and identify challenges water users face.

Language Arts

- Label maps to identify water users and show their locations in the Colorado River Basin. (writing)
- Create educational posters. (writing)

Social Studies Vocabulary

source, tributary, river basin, drought, irrigation, reservoir, habitat, conservation, wastewater

Materials

Social Studies Alive! Regions of Our Country

Transparencies 11A–11C

Interactive Student Notebooks

Lesson Masters

- Information Masters 11A–11E

Interactive Desk Maps

masking tape or blue tape

drinking water

4 opaque pitchers

large bucket or trashcan

3-ounce paper cups

Time Estimates

Preview: 30 min.

Experiential Exercise: 4 sessions (25 min. each)

Reading Further: 30 min.

Processing: 30 min.

Activity	Suggested Time	Materials
Preview • Connecting to Prior Knowledge • Building Background Knowledge • Developing Vocabulary	30 minutes	• *Social Studies Alive! Regions of Our Country*, Section 11.1 • Transparencies 11A and 11B • Interactive Student Notebooks • Interactive Desk Maps
Experiential Exercise Acting out how people use water along the Colorado River	*Phase 1* 25 minutes • Water use before 1800 (Steps 1–8)	• Information Master 11A (1 copy, cut apart) • Supplies: masking tape, water, 4 opaque pitchers, bucket or trashcan, 3-ounce paper cups (1 per student)
	Phase 2 25 minutes • Water use in the late 1800s (Steps 9–11)	• *Social Studies Alive! Regions of Our Country*, Sections 11.2 and 11.3 • Information Master 11B (1 copy, cut apart) • Interactive Student Notebooks • Supplies from Phase 1
	Phase 3 25 minutes • Water use in the late 1900s (Steps 12–17)	• Information Master 11C (1 copy, cut apart) • Supplies from Phase 1
	Phase 4 25 minutes • Water use in the future (Steps 18–22)	• *Social Studies Alive! Regions of Our Country*, Sections 11.4–11.10 • Information Master 11D (1 copy, cut apart) • Information Master 11E (1 transparency) • Interactive Student Notebooks • Supplies from Phase 1
Reading Further Analyzing the effects of water on people's lives in Supai, Arizona	30 minutes	• *Social Studies Alive! Regions of Our Country*, Chapter 11 Reading Further • Transparency 11C • Interactive Student Notebooks
Processing Creating posters	30 minutes	• *Social Studies Alive! Regions of Our Country*, Chapter 11 Summary • Interactive Student Notebooks
Assessment	30 minutes	• Chapter 11 Assessment, Lesson Masters • Chapter 11 Assessment, Digital Teacher Resources

Preview

1 **Connecting to Prior Knowledge:** Review with students details of the Southwest region of the United States.

- Assign students to mixed-ability pairs and distribute an Interactive Desk Map to each pair.

- Ask students to point to and name the states in the Southwest region. Then ask students to recall what they learned about the region in Chapter 10. Prompt students' thinking with questions such as these: *What places did you visit on the big rig tour? What geographic features did you learn about? What did you learn about the history of the region?*

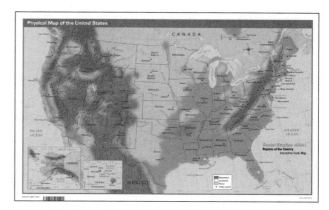

Interactive Desk Map

2 **Building Background Knowledge:** Help students understand that the Colorado River is a limited resource for the people who live near it.

- Project *Transparency 11A: The Colorado River.* Tell students that this geographic feature is the Colorado River. Explain that the Colorado River is one of the longest rivers in the United States.

- Have students read Section 11.1 in *Social Studies Alive! Regions of Our Country.*

- Project *Transparency 11B: The Colorado River Basin.* (**Note:** Keep the map projected throughout the activities.) Have students refer to this map or the duplicate map in Section 11.1 of their Student Editions as you ask these questions: *Where does the Colorado River begin? Where does it end? Do other rivers flow into the Colorado River? Which ones? Through which states does the Colorado River flow? Which international border does the river cross?*

Transparency 11A

- Help students become familiar with the geography of the region by having them use their fingers to trace the route of the Colorado River on their maps and having them identify the places and geographic features that the river passes by.

- Next, have students identify the impact of limited resources on people. Have students open their Interactive Student Notebooks to Preview 11. Read the instructions with students. Then have students complete the page.

- Afterward, have volunteers share their stories, briefly explaining what happened, how they felt, and why. Then discuss this question: *What is the best way to share something when there is not enough for everyone?*

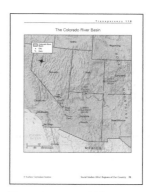

Transparency 11B

- Finally, tell students that in this chapter, they will learn how people have shared the use of the Colorado River, an important source of water for people in the West and in the Southwest. Explain that the Colorado River is an example of a limited resource. This means that there is not enough water in the Colorado River to supply water to all the people who want it.

3 Developing Vocabulary: Introduce key social studies terms—*source, tributary, river basin, drought, irrigation, reservoir, habitat, conservation,* and *wastewater.*

- Discuss each term before beginning the activity, using methods described in *Solutions for Effective Instruction.*

- Review each term again with students as it appears in the activity reading, and encourage them to use it in their writing.

Experiential Exercise

Phase 1: Exploring Water Use Along the Colorado River Before 1800

1 Prepare for the activities. Before class, set up the classroom and prepare materials.

- Arrange the classroom according to the diagram. Push all desks to the edges of the room. Place two parallel lines of masking tape at least six inches apart on the floor to represent the Colorado River. Place a large bucket or trashcan at the end of the tape to represent the Gulf of California. (**Note:** To create a more realistic or elaborate version of the Colorado River Basin, you might use blue electrician's tape for the river, desks to represent mountains or gorges, additional tape to create tributaries, and so on.)

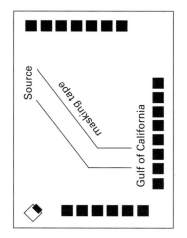

- Make a copy of *Information Masters 11A–11D: Phases 1–4 Role Cards.* Cut apart all the role cards. Each student will need one role card. If you have more than 28 students, make extra copies of the farmer, rancher, and city dweller role cards on Information Master 11B.

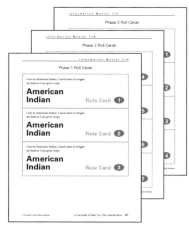

Information Masters 11A–11D

- Fill four opaque pitchers with water. To determine how much water you will need, subtract 4 from the number of students in your class. For example, if you have 28 students, pour 24 three-ounce cups of water into a pitcher. Pour the same amount of water into three additional pitchers, one for each phase of the activity. The goal is to have enough water for all students during the first three phases of the activity, but not enough for a full cup for everyone in Phase 4. If you use water jugs instead of pitchers, make sure they are opaque so students cannot see how much water they contain.

2 Introduce the Phase 1 activity. During class, tell students that they will learn how water from the Colorado River was used by groups of American Indians who lived throughout the West and the Southwest before the 1800s.

3 Have students "settle" the Colorado River Basin.

- Give one role card from Role Cards 1–3 on Information Master 11A, a piece of tape, and a cup to each of three students. Have them find a place along the "river" to settle. Make sure they are evenly spread out.

- Once students are in place, say to the class: *Let's see who lives near the Colorado River and why they need water.* Then have the three students, in numerical order, read aloud the sentences on their role cards that describe who they are and why they need water. After all three students have read their role cards aloud, have them tape their cards to their chests.

4   **Ask students to predict whether there will be enough water.** Show the class your pitcher of water and say: *This is how much water we can expect will flow from the Colorado River this year. I am going to fill the cup of everyone who needs water. Do you think there will be enough water?* The students will likely answer yes. Agree, and then say in a confident voice: *I am the Colorado River and will give each of you the water you need.*

5   **Demonstrate how the river flows.** Walk along the river, following the river's route, and fill each student's cup to the top with water. Do your best to pour the same amount into each cup without spilling. (**Note:** In Phase 1, you may want to pour too much water into the last cup, causing some to spill, and say: *The great river is unpredictable. Sometimes you can't control how much water will flow.* Tell students that flooding was often a concern and a problem for people living near the river in the centuries before dams were built.)

6   **Pour the remaining water into the bucket at the end of the river.** As you pour out the water, say: *Into the Gulf of California I go.* There will be plenty of water left, showing students that there was enough water for all those who needed it during this time period.

7   **Have students consume their water.** Tell students settled along the river that they may "use" the water they received from the Colorado River. To show people's use of water, students may now drink the water in their cups. If some students choose not to drink the water, have them pour it into the bucket. As they do so, you might say: *Here is more water that did not get used.* Have the students with role cards stay where they are along the river, as they will participate in all four parts of the activity.

8   **Debrief Phase 1.** Ask students who held role cards: *How did you feel during this part of the activity? How did you feel while the water was being poured into the other water users' cups? How did you feel when you received your water?* Then ask the class: *Who used water from the Colorado? Why did they need it?*

Phase 2: Exploring Water Use Along the Colorado River in the Late 1800s

9   **Have students enact the further settlement of the Colorado River in the late 1800s.**

  • Ask the first group of water users to stay in their places along the river.

  • Give one role card (from Role Cards 4–10 on Information Master 11B), a piece of tape, and a cup to each of seven additional students. Have them find a place along the river to settle, making sure they do not bunch up in any one spot.

- Place a strip of masking tape across the river, near the end that represents the mouth of the river. Tell students that this tape represents the creation of the U.S.-Mexico border after 1848. Make sure the student representing the Mexican citizen stands on the Mexico side of the tape.

- Explain to students that the settlers along the river represent the farmers, ranchers, city dwellers, and Mexican citizens living near the river during this time period. Note that these people are using the same resource as the American Indians who already live in the area—water from the Colorado River.

- Once students are in place, say to the class: *Let's see who lives near the Colorado River now and why they need water.* Have the newest water users read aloud the text on their role cards. These students should tape their role cards to their chests. Again, have those students who were already in place along the river restate who they are.

10 **Repeat Steps 4–7 from Phase 1, with the following modifications.** Note that because there are more water users, some students might question whether there will be enough water for all who need it. Ideally, students will become more concerned about the water supply with each phase of the activity. To help them gauge how much water is being used in each phase, be sure they are watching when you pour the remaining water into the bucket.

11 **Have students turn to the first two pages of Reading Notes 11 in their Interactive Student Notebooks to create maps of water users along the Colorado River.** Read the instructions with students. Have them read Sections 11.2 and 11.3 in their Student Editions. Then have them use the information from their reading and the activity to complete the maps and answer the questions below. Use Guide to Reading Notes 11 to check students' work.

> **Reading Strategy: Use Cloze Reading**
>
> If you are reading the text-book aloud to students, practice cloze reading by having students follow along. Stop at key words and have students say the next word.

Phase 3: Exploring Water Use Along the Colorado River in the Late 1900s

12 **Have students enact the further settlement of the river in the late 1900s.** In this period, many more people moved to the Southwest and began to build up the region.

- Have students with role cards return to their places along the river.

- Give one role card from Role Cards 11–20 on Information Master 11C, a piece of tape, and a cup to each of ten additional students. Have them spread themselves evenly along the banks of the river, especially at the top (the source).

- Explain to students that in this period, in addition to American Indians, farmers, ranchers, Mexican citizens, and city dwellers, there were also miners, business owners, recreational users, environmentalists, and power companies who wanted water from the river. (**Note:** You might need to explain "recreational users" and "environmentalists" to students.)

- Once students are in place, say to the class: *Let's see who lives near the Colorado River now and why they need water.* Have the newest water users read aloud the text on their role cards. These students should tape their role cards to their chests. Again, have those students who were already in place along the river restate who they are.

13 **Ask students to predict whether there will be enough water.** Show the class a new pitcher of water and say: *This is how much water we can expect will flow from the Colorado River this year. I am going to fill the cup of everyone who needs water. Do you think there will be enough water?* This time, some students will likely answer no, or be unsure. In response, say: *Since we aren't sure whether there will be enough water, what can we do to make sure all the users get what they need?* Have students share their ideas.

14 **Divide the river into two areas.** Tell students: *Just to be sure that everyone along the river gets some water, I'm going to divide the river basin into two parts and give exactly half of the water from the river to each part.* Lay a long strip of masking tape across the halfway point of the river.

15 **Create four dams along the river.** Tell students that to ensure that water users in both parts of the river basin will get their water, you will build four dams.

- Lay masking tape across the river in four places, with approximately equal spacing between each. (**Note:** While these represent some of the water projects—including the Hoover Dam and the Glen Canyon Dam—that were built between the 1920s and the 1960s, the placement of the dams in this part of the activity does not reflect their actual locations along the river.)

- Explain that each dam will temporarily stop the river water from flowing and will create a reservoir. Tell students that some of the water in reservoirs is kept for nearby water users; the rest is released back into the river.

16 **Pour water into each student's cup.** Tell students: *Now it is time for the river to flow.* Starting at the top of the river, walk with the pitcher of water to Dam 1. Stand on the tape and say: *I am holding water in this reservoir for five nearby water users.* Have the five closest students come to you, and pour water into their cups. Repeat the process at Dams 2 and 3. At Dam 4, do not give water to the Mexican citizen (Role Card 4); instead, tell him or her that the people of Mexico do not receive water from dams in the United States. Move away from the dam, toward the end of the river, and then pour water into the Mexican citizen's cup. There should be little to no water left to pour into the bucket. Make sure students notice this.

17 **Debrief Phase 3.** Ask students with role cards: *How did you feel during this part of the activity? How did you feel while the water was being poured into other users' cups? How did it feel when you received your water?* Then ask the class: *How did it feel to share the water this way? Do you think this way of sharing is fair or unfair?* Encourage students to explain their answers.

Phase 4: Exploring Water Use Along the Colorado River in the Future

18 Have students explore further settlement of the river in the future. Tell them that the amount of water in the Colorado is limited, but that more and more people need water from the river to live in the West and in the Southwest.

- Have students with role cards return to their places along the river.

- Give one role card from Role Cards 21–28 on Information Master 11D, a piece of tape, and a cup to each of eight additional students. (**Note:** If there are more than 28 students in the class, use the extra copies of the role cards for the farmer, rancher, and city dweller from Information Master 11B now.) Have students take their places along the river.

- Explain that in this time period, there are additional city dwellers, recreational users, and business owners who want water from the river.

- Once students are in place, say: *Let's see who lives near the Colorado River and why they need water.* Have the newest users read aloud the text on their role cards. Students should then tape their role cards to their chests.

19 Ask students to predict whether there will be enough water. Show the class the last pitcher of water and say: *This is how much water we can expect will flow from the Colorado River this year. I will fill the cup of everyone who needs water. Do you think there will be enough water for everyone who needs it?* This time, most students should answer a definite no, or be unsure.

- Tell students that since it looks as though people will need more water than the river will be able to provide, students will need to discuss what to do.

- Have students move into groups with other students holding the same role card (all American Indians together, all farmers together, and so on).

- Project a transparency of *Information Master 11E: Options for Sharing Water.* Have groups review the options and discuss which they think is best. (**Note:** The options are designed to get students thinking about possible solutions, especially conservation, which is the first option. You may want to allow students the choice of creating a fourth option that they think is better than those listed.)

- Read each option aloud and have students share their ideas about its pros and cons. After students have discussed all the options, conduct a vote to determine the preferred option. Then have students quickly return to their spots along the river.

20 Implement the winning option. Review the winning option with students. Then pour water in the students' cups according to that option. Use the dam system to distribute the water as needed. At the end of the river, note with the class how much water is left.

Information Master 11E

21 Debrief Phase 4. Ask students: *How did you feel during this part of the activity? How did you feel while the water was being poured into other users' cups? How did it feel when you received your water?* Then ask the class: *How did it feel to share the water this way? Did the plan you chose work well? Why or why not?*

22 Have students turn to the last two pages of Reading Notes 11 in their Interactive Student Notebooks to create maps of water users along the Colorado River and identify the challenges these users face. Read the instructions with students. Have them read Sections 11.4–11.10 in their Student Editions. Then have them use the information from their reading and the activity to complete the maps and answer the questions. Use Guide to Reading Notes 11 to check students' work.

Reading Further: A Home in the Grand Canyon

1 Project *Transparency 11C: Havasu Falls.*

- Ask these questions: *What does the photograph show?* (waterfall, pools of water) *Can you imagine people living right here? What might be the challenges of living here? What might be the benefits of living here?*

- Then tell students that these waterfalls are found in a remote area at the bottom of the Grand Canyon. They are called Havasu Falls. (These waterfalls are also known as Havasupai Falls.) A group of American Indians, the Havasupais, live near Havasu Falls. Other spectacular waterfalls and pools are also in this area. Many tourists come to the Grand Canyon to see these beautiful natural features.

Transparency 11C

2 Have students read Reading Further 11 in their Student Editions, either independently or in groups. Tell students that they will analyze the role of water in the lives of the Havasupais.

3 Have students turn to Reading Further 11 in their Interactive Student Notebooks to analyze the role of water on people's lives in Supai, Arizona. Read the directions with students and have them complete the page.

4 Debrief the activity with students. Ask these questions: *Would water affect the kind of home you would build? Would it affect the kinds of foods you would eat? Would it affect the jobs you would do? Would it affect how you had fun?* Be sure students can explain their answers.

Processing

1 Have students read the Summary in the Student Edition. Briefly review with students what they have learned about how people and businesses use the Colorado River.

2 Have students turn to Processing 11 in their Interactive Student Notebooks to design a poster about water use. Read the instructions with students. Then have students complete the page.

> **Writing Tip: Develop Vocabulary**
>
> Encourage students to use key social studies terms, as appropriate, when stating the challenges and solutions for future water usage in the Colorado River Basin.

- You might also want students to transfer their designs to large poster board so they can display their posters in the classroom.

- Have students share their poster designs (or the posters if they have created them) with the class. Encourage volunteers to explain how the text and images on the posters heighten awareness of the challenges people face about water resources in the future.

Assessment

Masters for the chapter assessment appear in the *Lesson Masters*. Answers appear below.

Big Ideas

1. B	4. C	7. A
2. C	5. D	8. D
3. B	6. A	9. B

Social Studies Skills

10. Colorado

11. Mexico

12. Gulf of California

13. San Juan River

14. Green River, Gila River

15. Glen Canyon Dam, Hoover Dam

Show You Know

16. The bulleted points can serve as a rubric for this item.

English Language Learners

As the class prepares to complete the Reading Notes, have students work with you, in pairs or small groups, to read all the text sections. Students can either read paragraphs aloud or follow along as the text is read to them. Incorporate frequent checks to ensure comprehension.

Students with Special Needs

While it is important for all students to be exposed to the power of an experiential exercise, it might be helpful to share with special needs students ahead of time how the activity will be structured. This may prevent students from feeling frustrated, uncomfortable, or intimidated as they try to find a space for themselves along the "river," or as they may possibly not receive enough water, or as they may not understand what their roles are. You might also pair students together and have them share roles. Encourage students to think about the important concepts presented and not be distracted by worrying about the logistics of the activity.

Enrichment

Now that students have learned about the Colorado River as a water source for many communities, have them research where the water in their community comes from. Students can use what they have learned about conservation along the Colorado River Basin, in both the chapter and the activity, to create a campaign encouraging others to conserve water in their own community. For example, students might create posters reminding people in the school to turn off water faucets completely when they're done using them, or asking community members to water lawns less frequently. Students' posters should explain why conserving water is important for the community.

Enrichment Resources

LearnTCI

Have students find out more about water use in the Colorado River Basin by exploring the following Enrichment Resources for *Social Studies Alive! Regions of Our Country,* at www.learntci.com.

Internet Connections These recommended Web sites provide useful and engaging content that enforces skills development and mastery of subjects within the chapter.

Enrichment Readings These in-depth readings encourage students to explore selected topics related to the chapter. You may also find readings that relate the chapter's content directly to your state's curriculum.

TeachTCI

For the teachers' resources listed below, click on Enrichment Resources for *Social Studies Alive! Regions of Our Country* at www.teachtci.com.

Biography Bank Hundreds of short biographies of notable people in history are available in PDF format for you to share with your students.

***Study Your State* Resources** Teaching directions and student activity pages (PDF format) will help you guide your students through researching their state.

Additional Reading Opportunities

The following books offer opportunities to extend the content in this chapter.

The Colorado River by Carol B. Rawlins (Danbury, CT: Franklin Watts, 2000)
This book focuses on the importance of the Colorado River, its geology and geography, and its ability to create hydroelectric power. This is a good resource for advanced readers.

The Hoover Dam by Leslie A. DuTemple (Minneapolis: Lerner, 2003)
Students learn how the Hoover Dam brings power and water to the Southwest. Charts, graphs, timelines, and color photographs accompany the text.

The Last River: John Wesley Powell and the Colorado River Exploring Expedition by Stuart Waldman. (New York: Mikaya Press, 2005)
Students learn about John Wesley Powell's expedition down the Colorado River as he studied the geology of the area. Dramatic illustrations, a foldout map that students can follow as they read the book, and excerpts from journals make this a valuable resource.

Water Power by Ian F. Mahaney (New York: Rosen, 2007)
This book explains how water can be used to create power. Dams, hydroelectric plants, and other ways in which rivers and oceans are controlled are discussed.

Read Section 11.2 in your book. Draw a simple symbol on the map below to show each group of water users. Label each symbol with the name of the group. Then answer the questions below the map.

The Colorado River Basin

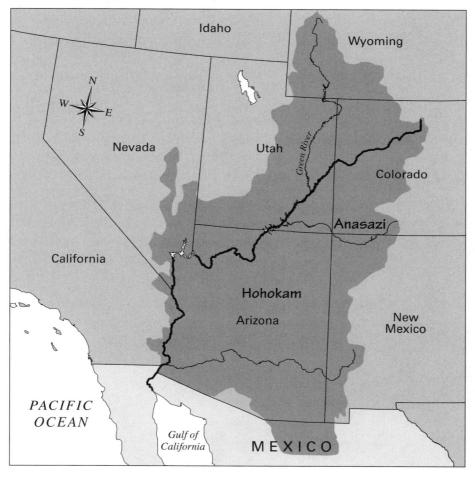

Was there enough water for all the groups of water users in the Colorado River Basin at this time? Why or why not?

Students should indicate that there was enough water for everyone during this time period.

If groups had to share the water, how did they do so?

Accept thoughtful responses. Students may indicate that people didn't have to worry about sharing the water, as there was more than enough water to meet everyone's needs.

Read Section 11.3 in your book. Then copy all the symbols from your last map onto this one. Next, for each new group of water users, add a simple symbol to the map. Label each symbol with the group's name. Then answer the questions below the map.

The Colorado River Basin

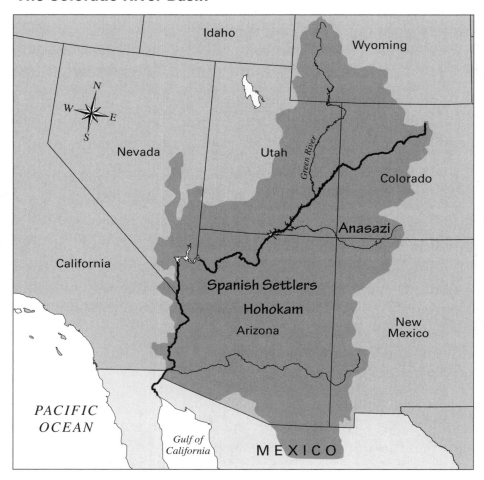

Was there enough water for all the groups of water users in the Colorado River Basin at this time? Why or why not?

Students should indicate that there was enough water for everyone during this time period.

If groups had to share the water, how did they do so?

Accept thoughtful responses. Students may indicate that people didn't have to worry about sharing the water, as there was more than enough water to meet everyone's needs.

Read Sections 11.4 through 11.6 in your book. Then copy all the symbols from your last map onto this one. Next, for each new group of water users, add a simple symbol to the map. Label each symbol with the group's name. Then answer the questions below the map.

The Colorado River Basin

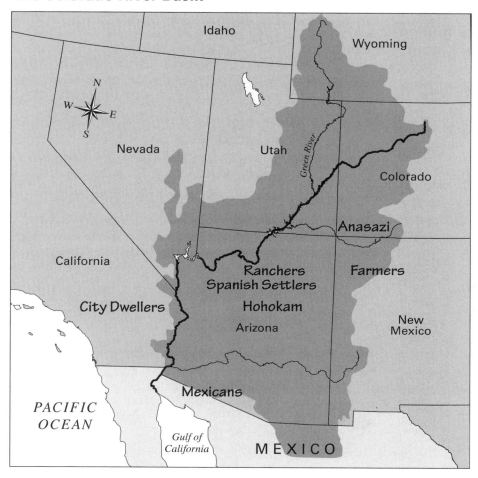

Was there enough water for all the groups of water users in the Colorado River Basin at this time? Why or why not?

Students should indicate that there was enough water for everyone during this time period.

If groups had to share the water, how did they do so?

Accept thoughtful responses. Students should indicate that people shared the water by using dams and reservoirs to control the flow of water in different places.

Read Sections 11.7 through 11.10 in your book. Then copy all the symbols from your last map onto this one. Next, for each new group of water users, add a simple symbol to the map. Label each symbol with the group's name. Then answer the questions below the map.

The Colorado River Basin

Was there enough water for all the groups of water users in the Colorado River Basin at this time? Why or why not?

Accept thoughtful responses. Students should be able to support their predictions about future water resources and water use with information from the text.

If groups had to share the water, how did they do so?

Accept thoughtful responses. Students may indicate that people will need to conserve water to have enough to share. Students may also write that dams and reservoirs will continue to help people share water.

Water is a big part of life for the Havasupai people.
It helps shape the way they live, work, and have fun in the Grand
Canyon. Suppose that you move to Supai, Arizona. Answer the questions
below to identify the ways in which water might affect your life there.

1. How might water affect how I will live in Supai?

   Accept thoughtful responses. Students may write that floods might force them from their homes.

2. How might water affect how I will work in Supai?

   Accept thoughtful responses. Students may write that the water allows them to irrigate their peach orchards or take tourists on canoe trips.

3. How might water affect how I will have fun in Supai?

   Accept thoughtful responses. Students may write that the water allows them to swim, fish, and canoe for fun.

4. What do you think will be the biggest advantage to living with the water in Supai?

   Accept thoughtful responses. Students may write that the biggest advantage of living with the water is having so much beauty around them.

5. What do you think will be the biggest challenge in living with the water in Supai?

   Accept thoughtful responses. Students may write that the biggest challenge of living with the water is the danger of destructive floods.

A Van and Airplane Tour of the West

What are the features that have drawn people to the West?

Overview

Students take a "van and airplane tour" of the West region of the United States. In the Preview activity, a Geography Challenge introduces students to the West. Then, in a Writing for Understanding activity, students listen to a tour guide and view nine images of places in the West. The tour stops at three sites, where students learn more through interactive experiences that teach key concepts of the chapter. Students then use their notes to write a letter about their excursions in the West. In Reading Further, students create a brochure to promote the Pacific Crest Trail. The letter-writing activity serves as the Processing assignment for the chapter.

Objectives

Social Studies
- Identify reasons why the West has attracted people.
- Apply map skills to locate nine important sites in the West.
- Trace the path of a tour through the West on a map of the region.
- Describe the physical and human features of the West.

Language Arts
- Gather information from an audio tour. (listening)
- Synthesize information into letter form. (writing)

Social Studies Vocabulary

pass, expedition, geyser, technology, gorge, sawmill

Materials

Social Studies Alive! Regions of Our Country

Transparencies 12A–12K

Interactive Student Notebooks

Lesson Masters
- Student Handouts 12A–12F
- Information Masters 12A–12E

CD 2, Tracks 11–21

Interactive Desk Map or large U.S. map

Time Estimates

Preview: 45 min.

Writing for Understanding: 4 sessions (varying lengths)

Reading Further: 45 min.

Activity	Suggested Time	Materials
Preview • Connecting to Prior Knowledge • Building Background Knowledge: Geography Challenge • Developing Vocabulary	45 minutes	• *Social Studies Alive! Regions of Our Country,* Section 12.1 and pages 186 and 187 • Transparency 12A • Interactive Student Notebooks • Student Handout 12A (depending on class size, 1 or 2 copies, cut apart) • Interactive Desk Map or large U.S. map
Writing for Understanding Taking a tour of the West and writing a letter synthesizing information about the region	*Phase 1* 60-minute sessions (3) • Introduction and Tour Sites 1–3 • Tour Sites 4–6 • Tour Sites 7–9 (Steps 1–8) *Phase 2* 45-minute session • Letter writing (Steps 9 and 10)	• *Social Studies Alive! Regions of Our Country,* Sections 12.1–12.10 and Summary • Transparencies 12B–12J • Interactive Student Notebooks • Information Masters 12A–12D (1 transparency, plus 1 copy per group of 3, of each) • Student Handouts 12B–12D (1 copy per student) • Student Handouts 12E and 12F (1 copy per group) • CD 2, Tracks 11–21 • Information Master 12E (1 copy per student or 1 transparency)
Reading Further Creating a brochure to promote the Pacific Crest Trail	45 minutes	• *Social Studies Alive! Regions of Our Country,* Chapter 12 Reading Further • Transparency 12K • Interactive Student Notebooks
Processing The letter-writing assignment serves as the Processing activity for this chapter.		
Assessment	30 minutes	• Chapter 12 Assessment, Lesson Masters • Chapter 12 Assessment, Digital Teacher Resources

Preview

1 **Preparing for the Preview:** Before class, make enough copies of *Student Handout 12A: Geography Challenge Cards* to give each pair one Geography Challenge card and have a few left over. (It is helpful to have a pool for students to pick from, in case other pairs are still using their cards.) Then cut out the cards. (**Note:** You may want to laminate the cards for future use.)

2 **Connecting to Prior Knowledge:** Introduce students to the West region.

- Tell students that the last region of the United States they will be learning about is the West. To help students see where the West region lies within the country, hold up the Interactive Desk Map or display a large map of the United States and point out the region.

- Have students look at the graphic organizer in Section 12.1 of *Social Studies Alive! Regions of Our Country.* Ask these questions: *What do you see? The dots on the map show the locations of places on the tour you are about to take. Where will you be going? How many states will the tour travel through? Which place on the tour are you most excited about visiting?*

- Project *Transparency 12A: The West Region.* Ask students to examine the collage of images of the West and then respond to the questions on Preview 12 in their Interactive Student Notebooks.

- Discuss students' responses. Tell students that they will be mapping features of the West. Afterward, they will meet Ms. Yoshida, who will take them on a van and airplane tour of the West so they can learn more about the region.

3 **Building Background Knowledge: Geography Challenge**

- Assign students to mixed-ability pairs. Pass out one Geography Challenge question to each pair.

- Have students open their Student Editions to pages 186 and 187 and their Interactive Student Notebooks to Geography Challenge 12. Review the directions with them. You may want to model the process for completing one question before you invite pairs to work independently.

- Monitor students' work, using Guide to Geography Challenge 12, found at the end of this lesson. After a pair finishes a card, have both students raise their hands to indicate that they are ready for you to check their work for accuracy and thoroughness. When necessary, instruct students to revise their answers. Remind pairs to exchange cards with each other until all pairs have completed most or all of the cards.

- Review with students the correct answers to the Geography Challenge. Have students look again at the maps of the West region in their Student Editions as you discuss the correct answers.

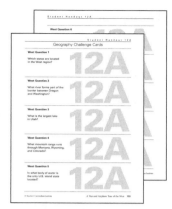

Student Handout 12A

Interactive Desk Map

Transparency 12A

4 **Developing Vocabulary:** Introduce key social studies terms—*pass, expedition, geyser, technology, gorge,* and *sawmill.*

- Discuss each term before beginning the activity, using methods described in *Solutions for Effective Instruction.*

- Review each term again with students as it appears in the activity reading, and encourage them to use it in their writing.

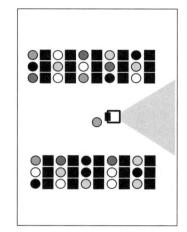

Writing for Understanding

Phase 1: Gathering Information

1 **Prepare for Phase 1 of the activity.** Before class, arrange your classroom according to the diagram. If necessary, prepare a transparency that shows students where they will sit. Make one copy per group of Information Masters 12A–12C to hand out at the appropriate tour stops. Also make enough copies of Student Handouts 12B–12F to give one to every student at each of the three corresponding stops. (**Note:** The "tour" portion of this activity will take about three hour-long class periods to complete—one period for Tour Sites 1–3, one period for Tour Sites 4–6, and one period for Tour Sites 7–9. You may want to prepare for only one period at a time.)

2 **Introduce the activity.** When students enter the classroom, welcome them to the Western Transport Hub. Explain that shortly they will be taking a van and airplane tour with their guide, Ms. Yoshida. Divide students into mixed-ability groups of three. Ask students to "climb into their vans" and take their seats. Tell students that on this tour of the West, they will see and learn about nine sites. They will stop at three sites to examine visual and written information about the history, economy, geography, and people of the West region.

3 **For each site on the tour, project the corresponding transparency and play the corresponding track(s) on CD 2.** The tour begins with *Transparency 12B: A Stop on the Lewis and Clark Trail* and ends with *Transparency 12J: Waikiki Beach, Honolulu, Hawaii.* The text of each CD track corresponds to a section of the Student Edition. Encourage students to read along in their Student Editions. To begin the tour, play CD 2 Track 11, "Introduction/Lolo Pass, Montana: A Stop on the Lewis and Clark Trail." (**Note:** Throughout the activity, pause the CD as often as necessary to ensure student success.)

4 **Have students identify nine important sites in the West by completing Reading Notes 12 in their Interactive Student Notebooks.** Students should trace the path of their tour on the map and describe the physical and human features of the region.

5 **After students visit each site, give them time to work on their Reading Notes.** Monitor students' progress.

Reading Strategy: Organize Resources

As students listen to the CD for this tour and follow along in their Student Editions, have them use sticky notes to mark new or interesting places in their text. Students can also take brief notes on the sticky notes to indicate what information is found there.

Transparencies 12B–12J

6 **Students will stop three times to interact with station information and learn about mining in Leadville, Colorado; changes in the Columbia River Basin; and tourism in the Hawaiian Islands.**

- For Tour Site 3, project a transparency of *Information Master 12A: Tour Site 3: Learning About Western Mining in Leadville, Colorado.* Pass out a copy of it to each group and a copy of *Student Handout 12B: Tour Site 3: Learning About Western Mining in Leadville, Colorado,* to each student. During Step 1, play CD 2, Track 14, "The Honest Miner's Song."

- For Tour Site 6, project a transparency of *Information Master 12B: Tour Site 6: Learning About the Decline of Salmon Along the Columbia River.* Distribute a copy of it and *Information Master 12C: Background Information About Salmon Along the Columbia River* to each group. Before Step 3, distribute a copy of *Student Handout 12C: Tour Site 6: Learning About the Decline of Salmon Along the Columbia River* and *Student Handout 12D: Information About the Columbia River Basin* to each student. After Step 5, project a transparency of Information Master 12C and read aloud to students the information about what people are doing to try to increase the number of salmon in the Columbia River Basin.

- For Tour Site 9, project a transparency of *Information Master 12D: Tour Site 9: Learning About Tourism in the Hawaiian Islands.* Distribute a copy to each group, along with a copy of *Student Handout 12E: Hawaii Trip Planner* and *Student Handout 12F: Attractions on Four Hawaiian Islands.* Each group will also need scissors and tape or glue.

7 **After the tour, give students time to complete Reading Notes 12.** Then have them check their Reading Notes and Student Handout answers against the Student Edition.

8 **To wrap up the tour, play CD 2, Track 21, "Summary."** Have students follow along in their Student Editions.

Information Masters 12A–12D

Student Handouts 12B–12F

Phase 2: Synthesizing Information

9 **Tell students that they will now write a letter describing their tour of the West.** Project a transparency of *Information Master 12E: Writing a Letter About the West* or give one copy to each student. With students, read the directions for writing a letter, clarifying the requirements as needed. Then have students write their letters.

10 **Debrief the activity.** Have several students read their completed letters aloud. Then discuss the following questions:

For students who do *not* live in the West:

- What aspects of life in the West did you most enjoy learning about?

- In what ways is life in the West similar to life in your region of the country? In what ways is it different?

- Do you think that you would like to live in the West? Why or why not?

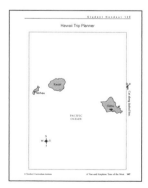

Information Master 12E

- If you were a tour guide like Ms. Yoshida, what one site in the West would you recommend that tourists visit? Explain.

For students who live in the West:

- What aspects of life in the West did you most enjoy learning about?

- Did you learn anything new that surprised you? What was it? Why were you surprised?

- Do you like living in the West? Why or why not?

- If you were a tour guide like Ms. Yoshida, what one site in the West would you recommend that tourists visit? Explain.

Reading Further: Exploring the Pacific Crest Trail

1   **Prepare for the activity.** Before class, collect books and materials about the Pacific Crest Trail.

2   **Project** *Transparency 12K: The Pacific Crest Trail.* Keep the transparency displayed during the entire activity.

- Ask these questions: *What do you see in the photographs? Where do you think these places are? Why do you think so? Can you think of things people might do to have fun here?*

- Tell students that the photographs show places along the Pacific Crest Trail and the John Muir Trail. Explain that they will learn about these trails and how they are special.

- Have students read Reading Further 12 in the Student Edition. When students finish reading, ask them these questions: *What sights might you see along the trail? Why do you think the trail might be important to people in the West?*

- Revisit Transparency 12K. Ask volunteers to identify the place shown in each photograph. Students can look at the photographs and captions in the Student Edition for help.

3   **Tell students that they will create a brochure to promote the Pacific Crest Trail to tourists.**

- Divide students into three mixed-ability groups. Assign one group the state of California, another group the state of Oregon, and the last group the state of Washington.

- Have students turn to Reading Further 12 in their Interactive Student Notebooks. Read the instructions with students.

- Give the groups time to peruse the materials you have collected on the Pacific Crest Trail. You might also want to schedule additional time for groups to use the Internet to find more information.

Transparency 12K

- Have each group create a brochure to promote the part of the Pacific Crest Trail that lies in the group's assigned state. Remind groups to focus on key attractions along the trail and why tourists should visit.

- Have students complete Reading Further 12 in their Interactive Student Notebooks.

4 Debrief the activity with students.

- Invite each group to present its brochure to the class. Have the California group present first, then the Oregon group, and finally the Washington group.

- Ask each group: *Why should people visit your state's part of the Pacific Crest Trail? What things might people see on your part of the trail?*

- Discuss with the class how each brochure might convince people to come to that state.

Assessment

Masters for the chapter assessment appear in the *Lesson Masters*. Answers appear below.

Big Ideas

1. D
2. C
3. B

4. A
5. D
6. A

7. B
8. D

Social Studies Skills

9. A

10. C

Show You Know

11. The bulleted points can provide a rubric for this item.

English Language Learners

In Phase 2 of the Writing for Understanding activity, modify the letter-writing assignment so students can more readily demonstrate their understanding of the chapter's content. Provide a structured framework so students can fill in their information without being slowed down by the writing. For example, give them sentence starters such as these:

One place I visited in the West was _____ .

It was interesting because _____ .

I would describe this place as _____ .

I learned that _____ .

Also, reduce the number of vocabulary words students must include, choosing only those words that you feel are most critical to student comprehension of the region.

Students with Special Needs

At Tour Stop 3, as groups complete their songs about mining life, encourage students to take the lead on creating the hand and body motions to accompany the lyrics. This will provide them with ownership of an integral part of the assignment and will incorporate a bodily-kinesthetic element to help them more easily recall and internalize the content.

Enrichment

As part of the Reading Further activity, challenge students to extend their learning about the Pacific Crest Trail. Have them create "travelogues" that show an itinerary that hikers along the trail might take from start to finish. Have students use information from their Student Editions, additional texts, or Web sites to research information about the trail. Ask students to cover the following topics in their travelogues: how many miles the trail is, when in the year travelers should begin the trip and why, what travelers should bring, and what they need to be careful of. Students should also map the distance a traveler can cover each week and write brief paragraphs to describe what can be seen along the way. Have students share their travelogues with the class to highlight the trail in greater depth.

Enrichment Resources

LearnTCI

Have students find out more about the West by exploring the following Enrichment Resources for *Social Studies Alive! Regions of Our Country,* at www.learntci.com.

Internet Connections These recommended Web sites provide useful and engaging content that enforces skills development and mastery of subjects within the chapter.

Enrichment Readings These in-depth readings encourage students to explore selected topics related to the chapter. You may also find readings that relate the chapter's content directly to your state's curriculum.

TeachTCI

For the teachers' resources listed below, click on Enrichment Resources for *Social Studies Alive! Regions of Our Country* at www.teachtci.com.

Biography Bank Hundreds of short biographies of notable people in history are available in PDF format for you to share with your students.

***Study Your State* Resources** Teaching directions and student activity pages (PDF format) will help you guide your students through researching their state.

Additional Reading Opportunities

The following nonfiction books offer opportunities to extend the content in this chapter.

National Parks (series) by John Hamilton (Edina, MN: Abdo, 2005)

This series presents information about the ecosystems, geology, geography, and animals of our national parks. Color photographs, maps, and diagrams add to these resources. Titles include *Glacier National Park, Grand Canyon National Park, Yellowstone National Park,* and *Yosemite National Park.*

Symbols, Landmarks, and Monuments (series) by Tamara L. Britton (Edina, MN: Abdo, 2005)

This series discusses important U.S. landmarks. Maps, charts, color photographs, and informational text provide students with insights into our national treasures. Titles include *Pearl Harbor, Angel Island,* and *The Golden Gate Bridge.*

Visitor Guides (series) by various authors (Mankato, MN: The Child's World, 2003)

Students travel to national parks and landmarks as they read simple text and view dramatic color photographs. Titles include *Welcome to Death Valley National Park, Welcome to Grand Teton National Park, Welcome to Hawaii Volcanoes National Park,* and *Welcome to Yosemite National Park.*

Use the spaces below to answer the questions on the Geography Challenge Cards. Write complete sentences. On the map, draw and label the feature that answers each question. Exchange your question with another pair of students until you have completed all the cards.

Question 1. The 11 states in the West region are Washington, Oregon, California, Nevada, Idaho, Montana, Wyoming, Utah, Colorado, Alaska, and Hawaii.

Question 2. The Columbia River forms part of the border between Oregon and Washington.

Question 3. Great Salt Lake is the largest lake in Utah.

Question 4. The Rocky Mountains run through Montana, Wyoming, and Colorado.

Question 5. The only U.S. island state, Hawaii, is located in the Pacific Ocean.

Question 6. Interstate 5 runs through Seattle, Portland, Sacramento, and Los Angeles.

Question 7. Three mountains in the West region are Mauna Loa, Mount Whitney, and Mount McKinley.

Question 8. Yellowstone National Park is in the Rocky Mountains.

Question 9.   Juneau, the capital of Alaska, is the Western state capital that is nearest one to Russia.

Question 10. Driving east on Interstate 80 and then south on Interstate 25 appears to be the shortest route between Salt Lake City and Denver.

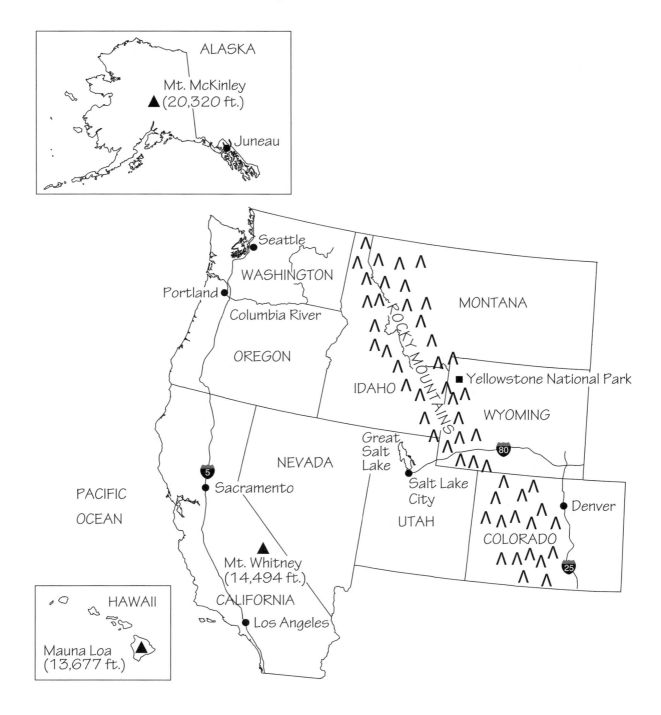

Your class is taking a van and airplane tour of the West region. The tour will take you to nine locations. As you move from site to site, draw a line on the map to show your route. After visiting each site, draw a symbol or an image at that location to show what you learned there.

Students' symbols and drawings for each site will vary.

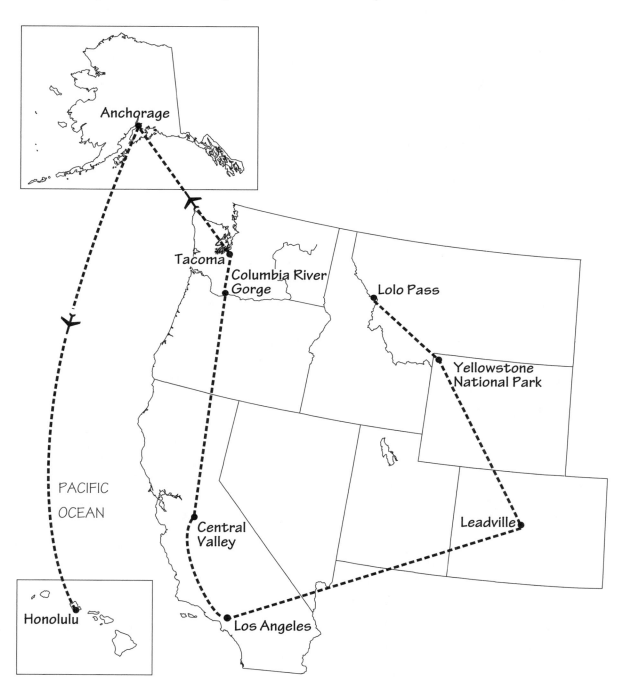

Cities of the West

What attracts people to the cities of the West?

Overview

Students learn about seven cities in the West. In the Preview activity, students analyze their favorite television commercials. In a Problem Solving Groupwork activity, students research, plan, and perform television commercials about cities in the West. In Reading Further, students plan television commercials to highlight the environmental appeal of Portland, Oregon. Finally, in the Processing activity, students use Venn diagrams to compare and contrast their own community with the western cities they like best.

Objectives

Social Studies

*   Identify characteristics of the geography, history, people, economy, and recreational activities of seven cities in the West.
*   Identify ways in which people in Portland, Oregon, keep the city beautiful and help the environment.
*   Compare western cities to students' own community using a Venn diagram.

Language Arts

*   Analyze television commercials for their purpose, content, and persuasiveness. (speaking)
*   Write a slogan and script for a television commercial to promote a city of the West, and perform the commercial. (writing and speaking)

Social Studies Vocabulary

mint, Mormon, oasis

Materials

Social Studies Alive! Regions of Our Country

Transparencies 13A and 13B

Interactive Student Notebooks

Lesson Masters

*   Information Master 13
*   Student Handout 13

CD 2, Track 22

Time Estimates

Preview: 25 min.

Problem Solving Groupwork: 60 min.

Reading Further: 30 min.

Processing: 25 min.

Activity	Suggested Time	Materials
Preview • Connecting to Prior Knowledge • Building Background Knowledge • Developing Vocabulary	25 minutes	• *Social Studies Alive! Regions of Our Country,* Section 13.1 • Transparency 13A • Interactive Student Notebooks • CD 2, Track 22
Problem Solving Groupwork Creating a television commercial about a city in the West	60 minutes	• *Social Studies Alive! Regions of Our Country,* Sections 13.2–13.8 and Summary • Interactive Student Notebooks • Reading Notes 13, first page (1 transparency, made from the Interactive Student Notebook page) • Information Master 13 • Student Handout 13 (1 copy per group of 4)
Reading Further Planning a television commercial about environmentalism in Portland, Oregon	30 minutes	• *Social Studies Alive! Regions of Our Country*, Chapter 13 Reading Further • Transparency 13B • Interactive Student Notebooks
Processing Comparing and contrasting communities using a Venn diagram	25 minutes	• Interactive Student Notebooks
Assessment	30 minutes	• Chapter 13 Assessment, Lesson Masters • Chapter 13 Assessment, Digital Teacher Resources

Preview

1   **Connecting to Prior Knowledge:** Help students analyze television commercials for their purpose, content, and persuasiveness.

- Ask students to think of their favorite television commercials. Have several volunteers describe these commercials to the class. After each description, ask students what the commercial was trying to get viewers to do. Have several students share their ideas.

- Ask students to think about the techniques, such as humor and jingles, that were used to help viewers remember the commercials.

- Have students complete Preview 13 in their Interactive Student Notebooks to analyze their favorite television commercials.

2   **Building Background Knowledge:** Tell students they will learn about cities in the West region.

- Project *Transparency 13A: Television Commercial Promoting the West* and play CD Track 22, "TV Commercial." Have students look carefully at the image and listen to the television commercial.

- After the commercial has finished, ask: *What does this television commercial want you to do? How does the commercial get viewers to want to move to the West? Does it use humor, music, or catchy slogans? From this commercial, would you be interested in moving to one of these western cities? Why or why not?*

- Have students read Section 13.1 in *Social Studies Alive! Regions of Our Country.* Ask them what they think they will learn about cities of the West in this chapter.

3   **Developing Vocabulary:** Introduce key social studies terms—*mint, Mormons,* and *oasis.*

- Discuss each term before beginning the activity, using methods described in *Solutions for Effective Instruction.*

- Review each term again with students as it appears in the activity reading, and encourage them to use it in their writing.

Transparency 13A

Problem Solving Groupwork

1   **Tell students that in this activity, they will identify characteristics of the geography, history, people, economy, and recreational activities of seven cities in the West.**

- Place students in mixed-ability groups of four. If necessary, prepare a transparency that shows who is in each group.

- Explain that each group will read and take notes about one important city in the West. Students will use this information to create a television commercial designed to make people want to move to that city.

> **Reading Strategy: Identify Main Ideas and Details**
>
> As groups of students read their sections in the text, have the groups practice the "Say Something" strategy by stopping at the end of a paragraph or subhead and taking turns saying something about what was just read.

- Assign each group one of the seven cities described in Sections 13.2–13.8 of the Student Edition.

- Have each group read the section corresponding to its assigned city.

2   **Have students record what they learned about their assigned cities on Reading Notes 13 in their Interactive Student Notebooks.** Help groups locate the sections of the Reading Notes that correspond to their assigned cities. Then review the directions with students and have groups work together to complete the notes.

3   **Have each group create a television commercial to promote its assigned city.**

- Distribute one copy of *Student Handout 13: Steps for Creating a Television Commercial* to each group. Assign students roles for the activity. Then briefly review the steps with students and answer any questions. As you review the handout, refer to the sample commercial from the Preview to give students concrete examples. (**Note:** Consider spreading the six steps over two days and reviewing only the steps groups will complete each day.)

- You might want to further explain the concept of a "gimmick" to students. Help them understand that a gimmick is a way of making products appeal to people through giveaway items, appearances by famous people, catchy songs, and other special efforts. For example, a commercial might tell the audience that a cereal company will give a gallon of milk to every person who buys a box of its new cereal. A commercial for running sneakers might feature a famous athlete saying how much she likes the brand of sneakers. Ask students to share examples of other gimmicks they have seen or heard in commercials.

- After groups complete each step on Student Handout 13, have them raise their hands to signal that they are finished. Check their work and initial the bottom of the appropriate page. Continue until groups have completed all six steps.

4   **Have the first group present its commercial. (Note:** If you plan to make a transparency of the first Reading Notes page for use in Step 5, the first group should present either Denver or Salt Lake City.)

- As the group prepares to present its commercial, have the rest of the students read the section of the chapter that corresponds to that city.

- Remind the presenters to use loud, clear voices when speaking and singing. When the group is finished, lead the audience in giving the group a big round of applause.

5   **Have students record notes about the city in the commercial in their Interactive Student Notebooks.**

- Project a transparency of the first page of Reading Notes 13. As a class, complete the notes for the first city presented, with students taking notes in their own Interactive Student Notebooks.

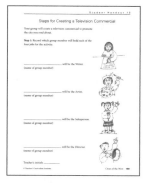

Student Handout 13

> **Speaking and Listening: Communicate Effectively**
>
> To help students communicate effectively during their presentations, create a rubric that includes guidelines for speaking and listening, such as:
>
> - Presenter speaks loudly and clearly.
> - Presenter uses eye contact when addressing the audience.
> - Each group member participates.
>
> Share the rubric with students as a reminder of your expectations.

- As you complete the notes, refer to the students in the group that created the commercial for that city as "experts." Ask these students to confirm the accuracy of the class-completed Reading Notes.

6 **Repeat Steps 4 and 5 for the remaining cities, allowing students to complete the Reading Notes for each section on their own.** (**Note:** Consider spreading the presentations over two days.)

7 **Have students use their Reading Notes and the groups' posters to select the city they would most like to live in.** Hang the posters around the classroom. Have students circulate around the room, looking at the posters and reviewing their Reading Notes as they select a city. Ask them to have one or two reasons to support their decisions.

8 **Lead students in a discussion about why they would like to live in the cities they chose.**

Information Master 13

- Have students stand in front of the poster for the city they selected. Then have the group standing at each poster discuss why they would like to move to that city. After discussion, ask a volunteer from each group to share some of the reasons those students would move to that city.

- After each group explains why they would move to the city they selected, read aloud the fact about that city from *Information Master 13: Surprising Facts About Western Cities*. Ask students if hearing this new information makes them change their minds about the city they selected. Encourage students to explain their answers.

- Close by having students read the Summary in their Student Editions.

Reading Further: Portland, Oregon: Green and Clean

1 **Project *Transparency 13B: Scenes of Portland, Oregon*.** Ask students the following visual discovery questions to describe what they see in the photographs:

- *What do you think each photograph shows? What sorts of scenes are these?*

- *What can you see people doing?*

- *Do you think these people are enjoying what they're doing? Why or why not?*

- *Do you think each scene is in a city or far from a city?*

Transparency 13B

Explain to students that the people in these photographs are enjoying a large rose garden, a massive urban wilderness area, and city bike paths, all in the city of Portland, Oregon. Tell students that Portland is known for being a very "green" city—one that includes a lot of natural beauty because the people there care about their environment. They keep it both beautiful and clean. Tell students they will read more about Portland in their Student Editions.

2 Have students read Reading Further 13 in their Student Editions, one page at a time.

- After the first page, ask: *What is the geography of Portland like? What attracted people to settle there?*

- After the second page, ask: *Why is Portland called the "City of Roses"? Why do people in Portland plant so many flowers?*

- After the third page, ask: *How do Portland's parks show that people there care about keeping the city green?*

- After the fourth page, ask: *In what ways do people help protect the environment in Portland?*

3 Tell students they will create television commercials to show Portland as either a "green" city or a "clean" city. Explain that students should consider what they have read and then decide, together with their original group members, whether to make a commercial about how people keep Portland beautiful or about how people there help the environment. Students may focus on one way or multiple ways that people in Portland do these things.

4 Have students use Reading Further 13 in their Interactive Student Notebooks to plan their commercials.

- Read the instructions with students. Tell students to follow the same process they used to plan television commercials about cities of the West. This time they will plan the commercials on their own.

- Have students complete the Reading Further pages to plan their commercials.

- When students have finished, ask volunteers to explain their commercials. Students should be able to say what the commercial wants people to know about Portland, what it might want them to do, and how it tries to make that happen (through humor, slogans, music, or other means).

- If you have extra class time, allow students to prepare posters for their commercials and present the commercials to the class.

Processing

1 Have students use a Venn diagram to compare their community to the city of the West they like best.

- Draw a sample Venn diagram on the board. Model how to use a Venn diagram by comparing two things, such as a cat and a dog or an apple and an orange.

- Have students turn to Processing 13 in their Interactive Student Notebooks.

- Read the directions with students. Then have them fill in things that are similar and different about the two communities.

- Ask volunteers to share their Venn diagrams with the class. Try to have each city represented at least once.

> **Writing Tip: Use Notes to Write Paragraphs**
>
> After completing the Venn diagram in their Interactive Student Notebooks, have students use what they have written as a springboard to write a paragraph comparing and contrasting their community with the city of the West that they chose.

Assessment

Masters for the chapter assessment appear in the *Lesson Masters*. Answers appear below.

Big Ideas

1. B	4. D	7. B
2. A	5. C	8. D
3. B	6. A	

Social Studies Skills

9. C

10. D

11. D

12. C

Show You Know

13. The bulleted points can serve as a rubric for this item.

English Language Learners

As groups prepare to create their commercials, explain each of the roles in more detail. Allow students to ask clarifying questions about each role. Then, before you assign other students' roles, have these students select the role they feel they would be most comfortable completing. Encourage each student to partner with another student in the group to complete the role.

Students with Special Needs

During the Processing activity, provide additional structure for students by offering categories that can be used as a basis for comparing their community to a city in the West. For example, the communities can be compared based on their geography, history, ways to have fun, and so forth. Consider providing students with a word bank as needed.

Enrichment

Review with students some of the persuasive techniques advertisers use to promote their products or services (humor, music, slogans, gimmicks, celebrity endorsements, etc.). Have students keep an "ad log" for a week, recording techniques used in any print, radio, television, or online advertisements they encounter during that time. For each advertisement, have students identify the type of product being advertised (food, clothing, toys, electronics), the persuasive technique used, and how the ad made them feel (such as more or less interested in the product). After students' logs are complete, have students draw conclusions and share how persuasive techniques are used in advertising. Discuss with students how being aware of persuasive techniques can make them smarter shoppers and consumers.

Enrichment Resources

LearnTCI

Have students find out more about the cities of the West by exploring the following Enrichment Resources for *Social Studies Alive! Regions of Our Country,* at www.learntci.com.

Internet Connections These recommended Web sites provide useful and engaging content that enforces skills development and mastery of subjects within the chapter.

Enrichment Readings These in-depth readings encourage students to explore selected topics related to the chapter. You may also find readings that relate the chapter's content directly to your state's curriculum.

TeachTCI

For the teachers' resources listed below, click on Enrichment Resources for *Social Studies Alive! Regions of Our Country* at www.teachtci.com.

Biography Bank Hundreds of short biographies of notable people in history are available in PDF format for you to share with your students.

***Study Your State* Resources** Teaching directions and student activity pages (PDF format) will help you guide your students through researching their state.

Additional Reading Opportunities

The following fiction and nonfiction books offer opportunities to extend the content in this chapter.

Great Cities: Los Angeles by Sabrina Crewe (Milwaukee: Gareth Stevens World Almanac Library, 2004)
Maps, photographs, a timeline, and interesting facts help take students on a tour of Los Angeles. Students will learn about the history, geography, and people of the City of Angels.

The Great San Francisco Earthquake and Fire by Michael Burgan (Mankato, MN: Capstone, 2008)
This book presents the story of the 1906 San Francisco earthquake in graphic-novel format. Colorful comic-book style illustrations and interesting text will motivate students to learn about this tragic event.

Pigs over Denver by Kerry Lee Maclean (Boulder: On the Spot Books, 2001)
Author Kerry Maclean wrote this fun ABC book with school children in Denver. It celebrates the sights and people of the Mile-High City through rhymed verse and colorful illustrations.

Springs in the Desert: A Kid's History of Las Vegas by Jonathan Peters (Las Vegas: Stephens Press, 2007)

Colorful illustrations and photographs and easy-to-read text teach students about the geography and history of Las Vegas. Students are introduced to the people who helped Las Vegas grow from a small town to a famous tourist destination.

Researching Your State's Geography

How has geography influenced life in your state?

Overview

Students research the geography of their state using maps, atlases, library books, and the Internet. In the Preview activity, they identify some of the most important geographic features in their state. In a Social Studies Skill Builder, pairs of students design a board game that includes the geographic features they identified. Afterward, they take turns playing each other's board games to test their geographic knowledge of the state. In Reading Further, students learn how archaeologists used geographic research to solve the mystery of an old American Indian village. In the Processing activity, they assess how successful their board game is as a teaching tool.

Objectives

Social Studies
- Identify the major geographic features of their state.
- Create a board game that details the geography of their state.
- Select an object for a time capsule from which archaeologists of the future could draw conclusions about the geography of where the student lives.

Language Arts
- Find information using maps, books, and the Internet. (reading)

Social Studies Vocabulary

physical geography, human geography, demographics, geographic inquiry process

Materials

Social Studies Alive! Regions of Our Country

Transparency 14

Interactive Student Notebooks

Lesson Masters
- Student Handouts 14A–14E
- Information Master 14

crayons or colored markers

cardboard, poster paper, and other materials for constructing games

a few board games and/ or copies of board game directions (optional)

Time Estimates

Preview: 30 min.

Social Studies Skill Builder: 2 sessions (45 min. each)

Reading Further: 30 min.

Processing: 30 min.

Activity	Suggested Time	Materials
Preview • Connecting to Prior Knowledge • Building Background Knowledge • Developing Vocabulary	30 minutes	• *Social Studies Alive! Regions of Our Country,* Section 14.1 • Interactive Student Notebooks
Social Studies Skill Builder Conducting geographic research and creating a board game	*Phase 1* 45 minutes • Learning about geographic research (Step 1) *Phase 2* 45 minutes • Conducting geographic research (Steps 2–7)	• *Social Studies Alive! Regions of Our Country,* Sections 14.2–14.6 and Summary • Interactive Student Notebooks • Student Handouts 14A–14D (1 copy of each per pair) • Information Master 14 (1 transparency) • crayons or colored markers • cardboard, poster paper, and other materials for constructing games • a few board games or copies of board game directions (optional)
Reading Further Exploring how geography helped archaeologists learn about Ozette	30 minutes	• *Social Studies Alive! Regions of Our Country,* Chapter 14 Reading Further • Transparency 14 • Interactive Student Notebooks • Student Handout 14E (1 copy per student)
Processing Assessing one's board game as a tool for learning geography	30 minutes	• Interactive Student Notebooks
Assessment	30 minutes	• Chapter 14 Assessment, Lesson Masters • Chapter 14 Assessment, Digital Teacher Resources

Preview

1 **Connecting to Prior Knowledge:** Help students identify major geographic features of their state that they can include on a board game they will create.

- Ask students to complete Part 1 of Preview 14 in their Interactive Student Notebooks to identify their favorite board game and explain why they like it.

- Next, create a T-chart that lists students' favorite board games on one side and reasons the games are successful on the other. Tell students that in this lesson they will be creating their own board games to learn more about their state's geography.

- Display a large map of your state. Then have students complete Part 2 of Preview 14 to identify and record the most important geographic features in their state—such as cities, the capital, major physical features, and key constructed landmarks.

2 **Building Background Knowledge:** Introduce the topic of geographic research.

- Introduce Chapter 14 in *Social Studies Alive! Regions of Our Country.* Tell students that in this chapter, they will learn how to study the geography of their state. Have them read Section 14.1.

- Ask students to examine the graphic organizer in Section 14.1 Ask: *What details about geography do you see?*

- Tell students that in this activity, they will use their lists of geographic features from Preview 14 as a starting place to research their state's geography and create a board game about it.

3 **Developing Vocabulary:** Introduce key social studies terms—*physical geography, human geography, demographics,* and *geographic inquiry process.*

- Discuss each term before beginning the activity, using methods described in *Solutions for Effective Instruction.*

- Review each term again with students as it appears in the activity reading, and encourage them to use it in their writing.

Social Studies Skill Builder

Phase 1: Learning About Geographic Research

1 **Have students learn and record information about geographic research.** Ask them to open their Interactive Student Notebooks to Reading Notes 14. Have them read Sections 14.2 to 14.6 and the Summary and record notes as they read. Use Guide to Reading Notes 14 to evaluate their responses.

Phase 2: Conducting Geographic Research

2 **Prepare for Phase 2 of the activity.** Before class, divide students into mixed-ability pairs. You may wish to prepare a transparency that shows students with whom they will work and where they will sit. Make enough copies of *Student Handout 14A: Creating a Board Game About Your State's Geography, Student Handout 14B: Creating a Fact Sheet and a Map for Your Board Game, Student Handout 14C: Writing Directions for Your Board Game,* and *Student Handout 14D: Designing the Pieces for Your Board Game* to hand one copy of each to each pair.

3 **Project a transparency of *Information Master 14: Board Game Example*,** and identify the key elements of a board game. Ask students these questions as they view the board game example: *What do you see? What are the features of this game? Do you think this would be a fun game to play? To make? Why might this be a good game to help people learn their state's geography?*

4 **Introduce the activity.** Pass out a set of Student Handouts 14A–14D to each pair. Review the project overview and requirements on Student Handout 14A. Explain that students will be filling in Student Handouts 14B–14D when Student Handout 14A directs them to. (**Option:** You may want to bring in board games or copies of the directions to a few popular games to distribute to students as examples.)

5 **Have students conduct research and create their board games.** Give pairs ample time to collaborate on and complete the project requirements. Monitor student progress.

6 **Have students display their games.** Once pairs have completed their projects, display them in the classroom and allow students to examine all the games.

7 **Have students play each other's games.**

Reading Further: Uncovering the Secrets of Ozette

1 **A few days before the activity, make copies of *Student Handout 14E: Collecting Objects for a Time Capsule* and distribute one to each student.** Tell students that they are going to choose an object or a picture of an object from home to bring to class. Review the directions carefully. Give students a deadline for bringing their objects to class. You might want to limit the size of the objects they bring to class.

2 **The day of the activity, display the objects and pictures that students have brought to class.**

Student Handouts 14A–14D

Information Master 14

Writing Tip: Crediting Sources

As students begin to search for facts about the geography of their state, introduce the idea of crediting sources in writing. Teach students to use a simple notation next to the fact to indicate the source for that information. For example, students could write a credit like this: *World Book Encyclopedia,* © 2008, Volume C, p. 155.

3 Project *Transparency 14: Artifacts from Ozette.* Ask the following visual discovery questions to help students analyze the images carefully and make some predictions:

- What do you see? Describe the objects in as much detail as you can.

- What might these objects be?

- What might be important about these objects?

- What might these artifacts tell you about the geography of the place where they were found? Do they suggest that the place is hot or cold? Might this place have forests, water, or both? Why do you think that?

4 **Explain that these are artifacts from Ozette, an American Indian village from long ago.** Tell students that long before Europeans came to North America, many American Indian tribes lived here. A tribe called the Makahs lived in the village of Ozette for thousands of years, in what is now Washington state. A few hundred years ago, the village of Ozette disappeared. For many years, people did not know if anything from the village could be found. Explain that students are going to read about Ozette and discover how a team of archaeologists used artifacts and geographic knowledge to uncover the secrets of Ozette.

5 **Have students read Reading Further 14 in their Student Editions.** Allow them to read independently or in small groups.

6 **To help students understand how archaeologists draw conclusions about life long ago by using artifacts and geographic knowledge, have them put together a time capsule for future archaeologists.**

- Tell students that to teach archaeologists in the future about the geography of where they live, they are going to put together a time capsule using the objects they brought to class.

- Ask students to open their Interactive Student Notebooks to Reading Further 14. Have them read the directions and complete the activity.

- Have students share their choices with the class.

- Put together a time capsule. You can bury the capsule or simply keep it on view for a while in the classroom.

Processing

1 **Have students open their Interactive Student Notebooks to Processing 14.** Review the directions with students.

2 **Have students play their game with their family or students in a lower grade.** They should then complete the page to explain how well the game teaches the geography of their state.

Student Handout 14E

Transparency 14

Assessment

Masters for the chapter assessment appear in the *Lesson Masters*. Answers appear below.

Big Ideas

1. B	4. A	7. C
2. B	5. A	
3. D	6. A	

Social Studies Skills

8. Possible answer: Albany grew up along the Hudson River, which gave people water and a transportation route to the sea and other parts of the area.

9. Possible answer: New York City has an ocean harbor and is at the mouth of a river that gives access to inland areas.

10. Possible answer: They wanted to connect Lake Ontario and Lake Erie to the Hudson River, for transportation of people and goods.

11. Possible answer: The canal probably increased trade and travel between Buffalo and Albany, making both cities much bigger than before.

Show You Know

12. The bulleted questions can serve as a rubric for this item.

English Language Learners

For the game-development process, assign ELL students to work with a pair of non-ELL students, allowing them to learn from multiple partners. As tasks are being divided, allow these students to choose the part of the game they would like to work on. Guide them toward the resources that will help them find the needed information most easily. Once they locate their facts, assist them in writing out the information as needed.

Students with Special Needs

As students read and record notes for Sections 14.2 through 14.6, have them work with a partner or small group to break the text into smaller chunks. Encourage students to use the Whisper Reading Alternating Paragraphs (WRAP) strategy, in which each student "whisper reads" one paragraph aloud while the other(s) follow along. This can be accompanied by the Radio Reading strategy, in which students summarize what they have heard after paragraphs are read aloud. Students then come to an agreement about the main idea of the text before moving forward. Students who are challenged by reading the text aloud can listen and participate in the summarization.

Enrichment

Have students use the geographic inquiry process to answer a question about their state that interests them. For example, if they want to learn more about how their state's population has changed over time, have them follow the inquiry process to pose the question(s) related to the topic, use library and Internet resources to find the appropriate data, organize the data in a meaningful way, analyze it, and pose possible responses. For the state's population, students might address how and why the population has changed, create a table showing the changes, and consider how the changes have affected or been affected by the state's resources and economy. Students can then present their findings to the class or to another class.

Enrichment Resources

LearnTCI

Have students find out more about studying the geography of their state by exploring the following Enrichment Resources for *Social Studies Alive! Regions of Our Country,* at www.learntci.com.

Internet Connections These recommended Web sites provide useful and engaging content that enforces skills development and mastery of subjects within the chapter.

Enrichment Readings These in-depth readings encourage students to explore selected topics related to the chapter. You may also find readings that relate the chapter's content directly to your state's curriculum.

TeachTCI

For the teachers' resources listed below, click on Enrichment Resources for *Social Studies Alive! Regions of Our Country* at www.teachtci.com.

Biography Bank Hundreds of short biographies of notable people in history are available in PDF format for you to share with your students.

***Study Your State* Resources** Teaching directions and student activity pages (PDF format) will help you guide your students through researching their state.

Additional Reading Opportunities

The following nonfiction books offer opportunities to extend the content in this chapter.

Got Geography! By Lee Bennet Hopkins (New York: Greenwillow, 2006)

This volume features appealing poetry about geography, travel, maps, globes, and exotic places. These meaningful poems will help students learn about Earth while celebrating geography.

Maps and Mapping by Susan C. Hoe (New York: Gareth Stevens, 2008)

Students will learn about the world through a series of maps that explore current issues of the environment around the world.

On the Map by Cynthia Kennedy Henzel (Edina, MN: Abdo, 2008)

This series presents information about the history of mapmaking, cartography, surveying, satellite imaging, and GPS technology. Students will also learn mapmaking and map reading skills. Titles include *Classifying Maps, Creating Modern Maps, Mapmaking, Mapping History, Measuring the Worlds,* and *Reading Maps.*

Read Sections 14.2 through 14.6, and record notes below.

14.2 What tools do geographers use to study a state's geography?

Possible answer: Geographers use maps, charts, graphs, and facts to study a state's geography.

14.3 How might geography have helped shape a state's history?

Possible answer: The land and its features help shape where people live and how communities grow.

14.4 How might geography have helped shape a state's economy?

Possible answer: Geography helps shape how and why people work the way they do.

14.5 What are six sources people can use to research their state's geography?

1. atlases

2. encyclopedias

3. the Internet

4. libraries

5. chambers of commerce

6. departments of tourism

14.6 What are the five steps of the geographic inquiry process?

Step 1. Asking geographic questions

Step 2. Acquiring geographic information

Step 3. Organizing geographic information

Step 4. Analyzing geographic information

Step 5. Answering geographic questions

Researching Your State's History

How can you learn about your state's history?

Overview

Students learn how to investigate their state's history. In the Preview, students identify and describe significant buildings from different eras in their state's history and brainstorm ways of researching their state history. In a Writing for Understanding activity, students research a building in their state and use it to tell part of their state's history. In Reading Further, students find out how a historian researched an important historic house in Philadelphia, Pennsylvania. The script-writing activity serves as the Processing assignment for the chapter.

Objectives

Social Studies

- Sequence events on a timeline.

- Identify primary and secondary sources of information.

- Identify details of the settlement, growth, and development of our states.

- Research a building in their state to learn about state history.

Language Arts

- Write a script. (writing)

- Read a script. (speaking)

- Record questions to ask while doing research. (writing)

Social Studies Vocabulary

primary source, secondary source, archive

Materials

Social Studies Alive! Regions of Our Country

Transparency 15

Interactive Student Notebooks

Lesson Masters

- Information Master 15
- Student Handouts 15A–15E
- Interactive Desk Maps or a large U.S. map

Time Estimates

Preview: 45 min.

Writing for Understanding: 2 sessions (30 min. and 60 min.)

Reading Further: 45 min.

Activity	Suggested Time	Materials
Preview • Connecting to Prior Knowledge • Building Background Knowledge • Developing Vocabulary	45 minutes	• *Social Studies Alive! Regions of Our Country,* Section 15.1 • Interactive Student Notebooks • Interactive Desk Map or large U.S. map
Writing for Understanding Researching state history by creating and presenting "talking buildings"	*Phase 1* 30 minutes • Learning about historical research (Steps 1 and 2) *Phase 2* 60 minutes • Conducting historical research (Steps 3–10)	• *Social Studies Alive! Regions of Our Country,* Sections 15.2–15.7 • Interactive Student Notebooks • Information Master 15 (1 transparency) • Student Handouts 15A–15D (1 copy of each per pair) • Student Handout 15E (1 copy per student)
Reading Further Exploring the mystery of the President's House in Philadelphia	45 minutes	• *Social Studies Alive! Regions of Our Country,* Chapter 15 Reading Further • Transparency 15 • Interactive Student Notebooks
Processing The script-writing assignment serves as the Processing activity for this chapter.		
Assessment	30 minutes	• Chapter 15 Assessment, Lesson Masters • Chapter 15 Assessment, Digital Teacher Resources

Preview

1   **Connecting to Prior Knowledge:** Introduce students to the concept of state history and help them begin sequencing events in their state's history on a timeline.

- Draw a long timeline on the board. Label the right-hand end with today's date and add the year of statehood near the left-hand end.

- Tell students that they will learn some ways to research their state's history. Explain the two dates on the timeline, and then ask if they know of any other important events in state history and when they happened. Add these to the timeline.

- Ask students what they would like to learn about their state's history, and list the topics on the board. (You may need to suggest a few ideas to get them started.) Discuss briefly with students where they might find information to answer these questions. Then help them understand one source of information about their state's history—historic buildings.

- Have students examine the graphic organizer in Section 15.1 in *Social Studies Alive! Regions of Our Country.* Ask students these questions: *What kind of building does this drawing show? Have you ever visited a building like this one? What is this building used for? What role might such a building have played in state history?*

- Tell students they will think about buildings from around their state. Explain that learning about different buildings can help us understand the history of a place.

- Have students turn to Preview 15 in their Interactive Student Notebooks. Read the directions together and have students complete the page. (**Note:** If students don't know how to identify the time period a building comes from, encourage them to draw the building anyway. If you know the era, you can help them by sharing that information.)

- Ask students to share the results of their individual brainstorming to create a class list of buildings that represent different periods in your state's history. Make sure the discussion results in the identification of at least 7 to 10 building styles that adequately cover your state's history—such as cabins, farmhouses, factories, schools, museums, skyscrapers, suburban homes, and apartment buildings—as well as landmark buildings in your state. You may want to use the same type of building more than once. For example, it might be helpful to include a farmhouse from the 1800s and a farmhouse from today so students can compare farm life in the two eras. (**Note:** As you progress through the lesson, add dates and information to the timeline on the board. Assist students in identifying important eras, dates, and events to place on it, along with simple sketches of the buildings erected during those eras.)

Writing Tip: Do Research Before Writing

Identifying important buildings and landmarks in your state's history may be difficult for some students. Help students search the Internet for important state buildings and landmarks from different eras. As a class, place these on the timeline to help students see how building styles have changed, or remained the same, over time. Your state and community Web sites are great places to begin this search.

2 **Building Background Knowledge:** Help students identify different sources for researching their state's history.

- Have students read Section 15.1 in their Student Editions.

- Have students brainstorm a list of sources, other than buildings, of information about their state's history. Encourage them to think about where they have learned about their state. Guide them to identify museums, statues, or historic sites in their state; books about their state; people who know about the state; and other possible sources of information about the state.

- Have students identify their state on their Interactive Desk Maps or a large U.S. map. Tell them they are now ready to become history detectives for their state.

3 **Developing Vocabulary:** Introduce key social studies terms—*primary source, secondary source,* and *archive.*

- Discuss each term before beginning the activity, using methods described in *Solutions for Effective Instruction.*

- Review each term again with students as it appears in the activity reading and encourage them to use it in their writing.

Writing for Understanding

Phase 1: Learning About Historical Research

1 **Have students read Sections 15.2 and 15.3 in their Student Editions to learn how and why people study history.** As students finish reading each section, ask them the questions below. Have students write their answers on Reading Notes 15 in their Interactive Student Notebooks. Use the Guide to Reading Notes at the end of this lesson to evaluate students' responses.

- For Section 15.2, ask: *How do historians explore the past?* Encourage students to give examples of primary sources and secondary sources.

- For Section 15.3, ask: *Why do people study history?* Encourage students to give specific examples of how studying history can help them learn about themselves and their state.

2 **Have students read Sections 15.4 through 15.7 in their Student Editions to learn about the settlement, growth, and development of our states.** As students finish reading each section, ask them the questions below. Have students write their answers on Reading Notes 15 in their Interactive Student Notebooks. Use the Guide to Reading Notes at the end of this lesson to evaluate students' responses.

- For Sections 15.4–15.6, ask: *How were most of our states settled? What are three ways that states became part of the United States? What drew people to some of the states?*

- For Section 15.7, ask: *What things influence a state's growth and development?*

Phase 2: Conducting Historical Research

3 **Tell students they will study the history of their state by researching the state's buildings.**

- Divide students into mixed-ability pairs.

- Project a transparency of *Information Master 15: Example of a Talking Building.* Explain to students that they will create "talking buildings," like the one they see here, to learn more about their state's history.

- Read the script on Information Master 15 with students. Then ask students to identify characteristics of the talking building shown.

4 **Explain to students how they will select and research a building to create a "talking building."** Distribute one copy each of *Student Handout 15A: Creating a Talking Building From Your State's History* and *Student Handout 15B: Researching Your Building* to each pair. Tell students they will use the Student Handout 15A as a checklist for completing the project. They will use Student Handout 15B to guide their research. Review the directions with students.

5 **Have pairs select and research their buildings.** Have students use classroom and library resources to find information about the buildings they chose. As you monitor students' progress, make sure that their research reveals the primary content objectives you hope to achieve. Initial each pair's Student Handout 15A as they complete each step.

6 **Have pairs draw sketches of their talking buildings.** Distribute a copy of *Student Handout 15C: Drawing a Sketch of Your Building* to each pair. Read the directions with students. Then have them draw a sketch that shows important characteristics of their building, its setting, and its use.

7 **Have pairs write scripts for their talking buildings.** Distribute a copy of *Student Handout 15D: Writing a Rough Draft of Your Script* to each pair. Read the directions with students and have them complete the page. Allow students time to edit their scripts and write their final versions on separate paper. Also give students time to practice reading their scripts.

8 **Have pairs create their talking buildings.** Distribute art materials to each pair for them to use to construct their talking buildings. You might want to have students use large boxes or poster paper to create their buildings, or work in miniature with craft sticks. Encourage students to show characteristics from their scripts on their buildings.

Information Master 15

Student Handouts 15A and 15B

Student Handout 15C

Student Handout 15D

9 Have pairs read their scripts to present their talking buildings. Distribute a copy of *Student Handout 15E: Notes Chart* to each student. Tell them to record notes on it as each pair presents its work. Then have pairs read their scripts and show their completed buildings to the class. Begin with the building from the earliest era in your state's history, and proceed to those that were built most recently.

10 Display students' work in front of the timeline of your state's history. Arrange the scripts and buildings along the timeline from oldest to newest. Give students time to examine the completed projects. Ask students to add information to the timeline on the board.

Student Handout 15E

Reading Further: Lost and Found

1 Project *Transparency 15: The President's House.* Ask the following visual discovery questions to help students analyze the image carefully and make some predictions:

- What kind of building does this image show?

- When do you think this building was built?

- What do you think this building was used for?

- What role might such a building have played in history?

Tell students that the image shows the President's House, a building that once stood in Philadelphia, Pennsylvania. Explain that they are about to read more about this building and its role in history.

Transparency 15

2 Have students read Reading Further 15 in their Student Editions.

- As they read, have students record, on Reading Further 15 in their Interactive Student Notebooks, the questions Ed Lawler asked in his research on the President's House.

- After they read, have students record additional questions that they would ask about the house themselves.

3 When students have finished reading, discuss the questions historians ask.

- Write each question—Lawler's and the students'—about the President's House on a sticky note. Then, on the board, write *Who, What, Where, When, Why,* and *How.* Point out that historians use these kinds of questions to guide their research.

- Help students sort the questions into these six categories. Ask volunteers to place each sticky note in the category where they think it best fits.

- Engage the class in discussion to confirm the placement of each question. Close by reminding students to keep these sorts of questions in mind as they research the history of their state.

Assessment

Masters for the chapter assessment appear in the *Lesson Masters*. Answers appear below.

Big Ideas

1. D

2. A

3. A

4. D

5. A

6. B

7. B

8. C

Social Studies Skills

9. This is a primary source, This diary describes things seen and experienced by someone who was there..

10. The diary states that Chambersburg, Pennsylvania in 1787 was a handsome little town with pretty stone and brick buildings.

11. Water power was used by the mills near Chambersburg.

12. Answers may vary. Students may note that travel in 1787 took a long time, used horses, and sometimes involved bad roads.

13. At the beginning of 1788, Lexington, Kentucky was a clever little town with a courthouse and some pretty good log buildings.

Show You Know

14. Students' interview questions should focus on the topics in the bulleted list.

English Language Learners

As the class shares ideas about different building types, assist students in creating an index card glossary to help them build vocabulary and connect words to visual images. Have students draw buildings such as a cabin, farmhouse, factory, school, museum, house, apartment building, or skyscraper. Alternatively, provide magazine or other images of buildings. Students should put one image on each index card and write or copy the word for the type of building it is. They can then punch a hole in the corner and use a notebook ring to make the picture-card deck. Students can use the cards to practice identifying and saying what each building is. Then they can mix up the cards and put them in chronological order as they learn about their state's history.

Students with Special Needs

As students are working on their scripts for a talking building, break the task down further so that students find it manageable yet still can take ownership of their work. Provide them with a few key resources from which they can easily find information about their building. Reduce the number of questions that they need to answer, and allow them to dictate or record their responses if they find that to be easier. Allow students to select which part(s) of the script they would be most comfortable reading aloud or find another meaningful way for the student to participate (such as introducing the group or showing the picture) if they cannot present in front of the class.

Enrichment

Have students extend their learning about their state's history by using classroom, library, and Internet resources to locate both a primary and a secondary source about someone or something in their state's history. For example, if they are interested in a famous person, they could find a speech, letter, or diary entry written by the person and also a biography or article written about the person. Then have them write a paragraph or two to explain what they learned about the person from the primary and secondary sources and how the sources differ from each other. Allow students to substitute a famous landmark or event for a person if they choose to.

Enrichment Resources

LearnTCI

Have students find out more about researching the history of their state by exploring the following Enrichment Resources for *Social Studies Alive! Regions of Our Country,* at www.learntci.com.

Internet Connections These recommended Web sites provide useful and engaging content that enforces skills development and mastery of subjects within the chapter.

Enrichment Readings These in-depth readings encourage students to explore selected topics related to the chapter. You may also find readings that relate the chapter's content directly to your state's curriculum.

TeachTCI

For the teachers' resources listed below, click on Enrichment Resources for *Social Studies Alive! Regions of Our Country* at www.teachtci.com.

Biography Bank Hundreds of short biographies of notable people in history are available in PDF format for you to share with your students.

***Study Your State* Resources** Teaching directions and student activity pages (PDF format) will help you guide your students through researching their state.

Additional Reading Opportunities

The following nonfiction books offer opportunities to extend the content in this chapter.

Primary Sources of the Thirteen Colonies and the Lost Colony (series) by various authors (New York: Rosen Publishing, 2005)

The books in this series use primary source documents to tell the stories of the thirteen American colonies. The lost colony of Roanoke is also covered.

Uncovering Our History: Teaching with Primary Sources by Susan H. Veccia (Chicago: American Library Association, 2003)

This resource for teachers offers information on a wealth of primary sources for use in elementary, middle, and high school classrooms. It also provides specific strategies for using primary sources with students.

Read Sections 15.2 through 15.7, and record notes below.

15.2 How do historians explore the past?

Possible answers

• by studying primary sources.

• by studying secondary sources.

15.3 Why do people study history?

Possible answers

• so we can understand the details of our lives

• to get clues about how the future may unfold

• so we can better understand who we are

15.4 How were most of our states settled?

Possible answers

- American Indians came looking for places to hunt or grow food.

- Europeans came looking for riches, natural resources, religious freedom and political freedom.

15.5 What are three ways that states became part of the United States?

Possible answers

- They were one of the original 13 colonies.

- They were the result of a 1787 law called the Northwest Ordinance.

- They were the result of a land agreement with other countries.

15.6 What drew people to some of the states?

Possible answers

- the promise of inexpensive land and open space

- dreams of riches

15.7 What things influence a state's growth and development?

Possible answers

- the state's natural resources, like soil, grass, gold, and silver

- the people who settle the state and what they do there

As you read about the President's House, record at least three questions that Ed Lawler asked during his research.

1. Possible answers: Who owned the house? Where was the house? What did the house look like? Who lived in the house? What went on inside the house? What were the stories of the nine African Americans who lived in the house?

2.

3.

After reading, record at least three questions that you would ask about the President's House.

1. Answers will vary.

2.

3.

Researching Your State's Economy

What do you need to know to understand your state's economy?

Overview

Students learn the fundamentals of a state's economy. In the Preview activity, they identify jobs they know and then relate these jobs to areas of economic activity in their state. In a Problem Solving Groupwork activity, students research one of eight economic activities and create a museum exhibit about that activity. Each figure in the exhibit "comes to life" to talk about the state's economy. In Reading Further, students learn about real-world work projects for kids around the country. In the Processing assignment, students analyze the economy of their own community and compare it with their state's economy.

Objectives

Social Studies
- Identify the primary economic activities of the state.
- Identify the three factors of production.
- Explain how the geography and natural resources of the state relate to the state's economic activities.
- Create a museum exhibit about an important economic activity in the state.
- Make choices about whether to spend or save money.

Language Arts
- Research and organize information on the state's economy. (reading and writing)
- Orally present information about one aspect of the state's economy. (speaking)

Social Studies Vocabulary

good, service, scarcity, market, factor of production, tax, budget

Materials

Social Studies Alive! Regions of Our Country

Transparency 16

Interactive Student Notebooks

Lesson Masters
- Student Handouts 16A–16F

poster paper

colored markers

blank stickers

Time Estimates

Preview: 30 min.

Problem Solving Groupwork: 3 sessions (varying lengths)

Reading Further: 30 min.

Processing: 30 min.

Activity	Suggested Time	Materials
Preview • Connecting to Prior Knowledge • Building Background Knowledge • Developing Vocabulary	30 minutes	• *Social Studies Alive! Regions of Our Country,* Section 16.1 • Interactive Student Notebooks
Problem Solving Groupwork Conducting economic research and creating a wax museum	*Phase 1* 45-minute session • Learning about economic research (Step 1) *Phase 2* 60-minute sessions (2) • Preparing wax museum exhibits (Steps 2–5) • Presenting and debriefing exhibits (Steps 6 and 7)	• *Social Studies Alive! Regions of Our Country,* Sections 16.2–16.7 • Interactive Student Notebooks • Student Handouts 16A–16F (1 copy of each per group of 4) • poster paper • colored markers • blank stickers (4 per group)
Reading Further Exploring economic choices in Enterprise City	30 minutes	• *Social Studies Alive! Regions of Our Country,* Chapter 16 Reading Further • Transparency 16 • Interactive Student Notebooks • blank stickers
Processing Comparing the economy of the community with the economy of the state	30 minutes	• Interactive Student Notebooks • poster paper • blank stickers (3 per student)
Assessment	30 minutes	• Chapter 16 Assessment, Lesson Masters • Chapter 16 Assessment, Digital Teacher Resources

Preview

1 **Connecting to Prior Knowledge:** Have students identify jobs they know.

- Ask students to complete Part 1 of Preview 16 in their Interactive Student Notebooks to identify some jobs they know about in their state.

- Create a master list of jobs. Follow these steps:

  - Form a large circle with your students. Announce that students will pantomime the popular jobs they have listed in their notebooks.

  - Demonstrate a pantomime by pretending to do a job such as hauling in a big fish. Then ask students to guess the type of job you have pantomimed.

  - Ask volunteers to pantomime jobs while other students guess the types of jobs being performed. On the board or on a piece of poster paper, add the job each volunteer performs to a class list of "Jobs in Our State." Continue until all the jobs that students listed in their notebooks have been pantomimed.

2 **Building Background Knowledge:** Introduce the topic of economic research.

- Tell students that in this chapter, they will learn how to understand their state's economy. Have them read Section 16.1 in *Social Studies Alive! Regions of Our Country*.

- Introduce the graphic organizer in Section 16.1. Ask students to examine the illustrations. Ask: *What do you see? What kind of work do these people do? How might these people contribute to the economy of their state?*

- Discuss how the "Jobs in Our State" master list you created relates to the economic activities in the state, pointing out relationships among the jobs on the list. For example, farmers rely on truckers to take their crops to market, and they need people at manufacturing plants to transform their crops into something consumers will buy. They also need grocers to market and sell their produce. All of these jobs relate to food production.

- Work with students to develop a list of eight key economic activities in the state. High technology, agriculture, construction, and tourism are four possible examples. In Part 2 of Preview 16 in their Interactive Notebooks, students should list these eight economic activities.

3 **Developing Vocabulary:** Introduce key social studies terms—*good, service, scarcity, market, factor of production, tax,* and *budget.*

- Discuss each term before beginning the activity, using methods described in *Solutions for Effective Instruction*.

- Review each term again with students as it appears in the activity reading, and encourage them to use it in their writing.

Problem Solving Groupwork

Phase 1: Learning About Economic Research

1 Have students learn information about economics, including how to identify the elements of an economy and explain the forces that affect their state's economic activities. Break the reading into two parts, with discussion in between, to ensure students' comprehension of the content.

- Have students read Sections 16.2 through 16.4 in their Student Editions. Ask them to record notes on Reading Notes 16 in their Interactive Student Notebooks as they read.

- Use Guide to Reading Notes 16 at the end of this lesson to evaluate their responses, and answer any questions students may have.

- Repeat the steps above for Sections 16.5 through 16.7.

Phase 2: Conducting Economic Research for a Museum Exhibit

2 Prepare for Phase 2 of the activity. Divide students into mixed-ability groups of four. You may want to prepare a transparency that shows assigned student groups and seating arrangements. Assign each group one of the eight economic activities from the list developed during the Preview. Make enough copies of *Student Handouts 16A–16F: Creating a Wax Museum Exhibit About Your State's Economy* to give one copy of each handout to each group.

3 Introduce students to the museum exhibit activity. Explain that they will be learning about their state's economy by creating "interactive wax museums." Ask students whether they have ever visited a real wax museum. Tell them that the wax museum exhibits they will create are different from those they may have seen or heard about. In this project, students will create figures that "come to life" to teach the class about the state's economic activities.

4 Distribute a set of Student Handouts 16A–16F to each group for use in researching their assigned economic activity. Give each group poster paper and markers. Assign roles for the project and review the project overview and requirements with students. (**Note:** You may want to set deadlines for each of the steps required to complete the project. In addition, you may want to create a grading rubric to hand out to students before they begin working.)

5 Monitor student progress. Give students time to complete each step of the project. As you monitor their progress, make sure that the museum exhibits are representative of the state's economy and that students' research reveals the content objectives you hope to achieve.

6 Have groups present their exhibits.

- Ask the first presenting group to make sure that they have their "buttons" attached to their shoulders. Then have them post their backdrop on a wall in the classroom, step in front of the backdrop, and freeze into position.

- Gently press one of the buttons to demonstrate to students how to interact with the exhibit.

> ### Vocabulary Development: Create Category Maps
>
> After students read Sections 16.1 through 16.7 in their Student Editions, have them use economic terms from the reading to create category maps. Students should use the list of jobs generated in Part 1 of the Preview to map jobs to each economic term. For example, *grocer, shop owner,* and *salesperson* could cluster around the economic term *retail.*

Student Handouts 16A–16F

- Ask for volunteers to press a button to bring a character to life.

- After each performer in the group has presented, talk about the importance of that economic activity to the state's economy.

7 **Debrief the presentations.** Ask students these questions:

- What did you like best about this activity?

- What did you like least?

- What facts about the state's economy did you learn from the presentations?

- What are the most important economic activities in our state?

- If you had to choose to work in one of our state's economic activities, which activity would you choose and why?

Reading Further: Doing Real Work in the Real World

1 **Prepare for the Reading Further activity.** Using post-its or write-on stickers, put prices on classroom items, such as books, art materials, furniture, and classroom pets. Aim for a mix of items that cost $20, $10, $5, and $1.

2 **Project *Transparency 16: Enterprise City.*** Ask the following visual discovery questions to help students analyze the image carefully and make some predictions:

- What do you see? Describe the image in as much detail as you can.

- What words do you see on the image?

- It says "Enterprise City" in the middle of this image. What kind of city could this be? Where does it seem to be located?

- What might be important about this "city"?

- Tell students that in their books they will learn more about this special city and other places where students do real-world work.

3 **Have students read Reading Further 16 in their Student Editions.** Allow them to read independently or in small groups.

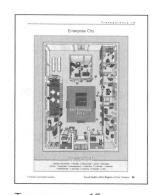

Transparency 16

4 **Discuss with students the examples they read of kids doing real-world work.** Ask students to explain what each experience taught kids about real-world work.

5 **Have students open their Interactive Student Notebooks to Reading Further 16.** Read the directions with students. You might want to brainstorm with students types of real-world work experiences they may have had, such as helping with fundraising and volunteering. Have students complete the page.

6 **When students have completed their pages, discuss their experiences doing real-world work.** Ask volunteers to describe the kinds of jobs they did. Encourage them to explain what they learned from their experiences.

Processing

1 **Begin creating a comparison chart about the economies of your community and your state.** On a large sheet of poster paper, list the eight economic activities that were the basis for the wax museum exhibits. Then tell students that you want to find out how the economy of your community is similar to and different from your state's economy.

2 **Brainstorm with students to complete the chart.** Ask students to think of jobs that three adults in their community are involved in. Then give each student three stickers. Help students write labels on the stickers to classify each job, creating additional categories if necessary. Ask students to place their stickers on the poster paper, next to the economic activities that match the jobs they listed.

3 **Discuss the chart.** Once the chart is complete, discuss these questions: *How is our community's economy similar to our state's economy? How is it different from our state's economy?*

4 **Have students open their Interactive Student Notebooks to Processing 16.** Review the directions. Then have students complete the page to summarize what they have learned about the economies of their community and their state.

Assessment

Masters for the chapter assessment appear in the *Lesson Masters*. Answers appear below.

Big Ideas

1. D
2. C
3. D
4. A
5. C
6. B
7. B
8. A

Social Studies Skills

9. from pay for working in the factory

10. wood, trees, forests

11. Possible answers: The restaurant needs tables and chairs so that people will pay to eat there. When the restaurant buys chairs from the factory, the factory can pay Jess, and Jess can sepend money at the restaurant.

12 Possible answers: work in the factory, work in the restaurant (also accept specific factory or restaurant jobs such as cook, waiter)

13. labor

14. Arrows should go clockwise from person to restaurant, from restaurant to factory, and from factory to person.

Show You Know

15. The bulleted points can serve as a rubric for this item.

English Language Learners

As groups work on creating their museum exhibits and writing their scripts, modify the requirements as appropriate to meet students' needs. For example, allow students to use one sentence, rather than four, to answer their wax figure's question, or answer an alternative question designed to simply elicit what type of worker they are and what they do.

Students with Special Needs

Before introducing the wax museum activity to the whole class, preview the project with students so that they know what to expect and can ask clarifying questions individually or in a small group. Allow them the opportunity to select the groupwork role that they feel they would attain success with and would be comfortable doing. Then assist them in identifying what steps they should follow to complete the project. As necessary, have students check in more frequently with you so you can assess their progress, enabling them to experience success along the way.

Enrichment

A wide variety of children's books that illustrate economic concepts have been published. Provide a selection of titles, such as those suggested in the Additional Reading Opportunities section in this Lesson Guide, or ask a school librarian for recommendations. Have students select and read a book and identify any economic activities evident in the story that relate to one of the important economic activities found in their state. Students can draw the activity and caption their pictures appropriately.

Enrichment Resources

LearnTCI

Have students find out more about economics and researching the economy of their state by exploring the following Enrichment Resources for *Social Studies Alive! Regions of Our Country,* at www.learntci.com.

Internet Connections These recommended Web sites provide useful and engaging content that enforces skills development and mastery of subjects within the chapter.

Enrichment Readings These in-depth readings encourage students to explore selected topics related to the chapter. You may also find readings that relate the chapter's content directly to your state's curriculum.

TeachTCI

For the teachers' resources listed below, click on Enrichment Resources for *Social Studies Alive! Regions of Our Country* at www.teachtci.com.

Biography Bank Hundreds of short biographies of notable people in history are available in PDF format for you to share with your students.

***Study Your State* Resources** Teaching directions and student activity pages (PDF format) will help you guide your students through researching their state.

Additional Reading Opportunities

The following nonfiction books offer opportunities to extend the content in this chapter.

Beyond the Lemonade Stand by Bill Rancic (Chanhassen: MN, 2006)

Students will learn about the principles of business, from business models to products. Ideas about starting businesses and advice from successful business-people are also presented.

The New Totally Awesome Business Book for Kids, revised third edition by Arthur & Rose Bochner (New York: Newmarket, 2007)

Students will learn about record keeping, research, marketing, working with others, and advertising. Students will be able to see how a business operates by planning a small business themselves.

Read Sections 16.2 through 16.7 in your book and complete the notes below.

16.2 What are the three basic economic questions that people, businesses, and governments seek to answer?

1. What goods and services should be produced?

2. How should goods and services be produced?

3. Who will consume these goods and services?

16.3 How does an economist define the word *market*?
A market is any place where economic activity occurs.

16.4 List the three factors of production.

1. land

2. capital

3. labor

16.5 List two things consumers can do to use their money wisely.

1. make a budget

2. save

16.6 What are two things that help shape the way an economy grows and develops?

1. natural resources

2. climate

16.7 List five economic activities that are common in the United States.

1. agriculture

2. manufacturing

3. retail

4. government

5 service

Researching Your State's Government

How does your state's government work?

Overview

Students learn about their state's government. In the Preview activity, students list state problems and propose solutions. In a Writing for Understanding activity, they play a game to learn the sequence of a state's legislative process. After researching their state's government, they write a letter to a state leader asking for help creating a new law to solve a problem. In Reading Further, they learn about a group of student citizens who helped create a new law. The writing assignment serves as the Processing activity for the chapter.

Objectives

Social Studies

- Identify state problems and propose solutions.
- Define the three branches of state government and what each branch does.
- Identify some rights and responsibilities of citizens.

Language Arts

- Describe the process of how an idea becomes a state law. (writing)
- Write a letter to a state leader (writing)

Social Studies Vocabulary

federal government, state government, citizen, local government, system of checks and balances, republic, legislator, bill, state constitution, right of free petition

Materials

Social Studies Alive! Regions of Our Country

Transparency 17

Placards 17A–17G (2 sets)

Interactive Student Notebooks

Lesson Masters

- Information Master 17
- Student Handouts 17A and 17B

Time Estimates

Preview: 30 min.

Writing for Understanding: 2 sessions (60 min. each)

Reading Further: 30 min.

Activity	Suggested Time	Materials
Preview • Connecting to Prior Knowledge • Building Background Knowledge • Developing Vocabulary	30 minutes	• *Social Studies Alive! Regions of Our Country,* Section 17.1 • Interactive Student Notebooks
Writing for Understanding Learning about state government and writing a letter to a state leader	*Phase 1* 60 minutes • Learning about state government (Steps 1–3) *Phase 2* 60 minutes • Researching your state's government and writing a letter to a state leader (Steps 4–7)	• *Social Studies Alive! Regions of Our Country,* Sections 17.2–17.7 • Placards 17A–17G (2 sets) • Interactive Student Notebooks • Information Master 17 (1 transparency) • Student Handouts 17A and 17B (1 copy of each per student)
Reading Further Exploring how student citizens can make a difference	30 minutes	• *Social Studies Alive! Regions of Our Country,* Chapter 17 Reading Further • Transparency 17 • Interactive Student Notebooks
Processing The writing assignment serves as the Processing activity for this chapter.		
Assessment	30 minutes	• Chapter 17 Assessment, Lesson Masters • Chapter 17 Assessment, Digital Teacher Resources

Preview

1 **Connecting to Prior Knowledge:** Have students develop a list of problems in their state.

- Open a class discussion by explaining that every state has problems. Give a few examples, such as traffic congestion and air pollution, and ask students to brainstorm some of the problems in your state. (**Note:** You may wish to collect articles, images from magazines or newspapers, or video clips that illustrate problems specific to your state—such as homelessness, pollution, aging highways, or decaying schools—and allow time for students to explore the material.)

- Have students open their Interactive Student Notebooks to Preview 17. Review the directions with them. Divide students into mixed-ability pairs and have them complete Part 1 together to identify four problems.

- Ask pairs to share the problems they have identified. Record their ideas on a transparency or chart paper. Then have students write the additional problems from the class list in Part 2 of Preview 17.

2 **Building Background Knowledge:** Introduce the idea that state leaders propose laws to help solve problems. Have students practice proposing solutions to problems.

- Explain that once a problem is identified, the next step is to develop a possible solution. Direct pairs to complete Part 3 of Preview 17 in their Interactive Student Notebooks.

- Ask pairs to share their solution proposals with the class. Point out that one problem might have more than one solution. Tell students that in this lesson, they will be proposing solutions to problems in their state. They will also write letters they could send to state leaders to ask for help turning their ideas into laws.

- Have students read Section 17.1 in *Social Studies Alive! Regions of Our Country.*

- Ask students to examine the graphic organizer in Section 17.1. Ask them these questions: *What do you see? Have you ever visited a building like the one you see here?*

3 **Developing Vocabulary:** Introduce key social studies terms—*federal government, state government, citizen, local government, system of checks and balances, republic, legislator, bill, state constitution,* and *right of free petition.*

- Discuss each term before beginning the activity, using methods described in *Solutions for Effective Instruction.*

- Review each term again with students as it appears in the activity reading, and encourage them to use it in their writing.

Reading Strategy: Summarize

If students read through articles from newspapers and magazines, have them summarize what they read. Tell them to write a $2.00 summary, in which each word costs 10 cents. This will help them condense what they have to say about what they read.

Writing for Understanding

Phase 1: Learning About State Government

1 **Prepare for Phase 1 of the activity.** Before class, divide students into mixed-ability pairs. Then assign pairs to one of two teams for playing the game later in the activity. You may wish to prepare a transparency that shows students with whom they will work and where they will sit.

2 **Have pairs read and record information about state government, including how to define the three branches of government and identify rights and responsibilities of citizens.** Break the reading into two parts, with discussion in between, to ensure student comprehension of the content.

   - Have students read Sections 17.2 through 17.4 in their Student Editions. Ask them to record notes on Reading Notes 17 in their Interactive Student Notebooks as they read.

   - Use Guide to Reading Notes 17 at the end of this lesson to evaluate their responses, and answer any questions students have.

   - Repeat the steps above for Sections 17.5 through 17.7.

3 **To help students understand the typical sequence of steps in a state's legislative process, have them play the *How an Idea Becomes a Law* game.** (**Note:** Make sure students have closed their Student Editions before you begin the game, so they are not looking at the diagram in Section 17.6 as they play.)

   - Tell students that they will play a game to learn more about how an idea becomes a law in many states. Have student pairs assemble into two teams.

   - Display a transparency of *Information Master 17: The Laptop Law*. Read the page aloud to students to prepare them to play the game.

   - Distribute one set of *Placards 17A–17G: How a Bill Becomes a Law* to each team (one placard to each pair). (**Note:** If you have too many placards, allow individual students to hold one placard each as necessary. If you have too few placards, allow students to work in larger groups.) Explain that each placard shows one step in the process of how an idea becomes a law.

   - Explain that pairs on each team must figure out the correct sequence of placards and line up accordingly with their placards in hand. Once a team is in agreement about the sequence, have all team members silently raise their hands.

   - When both teams are ready, ask the teams to compare what they have done by holding up their placards and facing the other team. Here is the correct sequence:

   Placard 17C: Discovering a Problem
   Placard 17G: A Legislator Writes the "Laptop Bill"
   Placard 17A: A Legislative Committee Discusses the "Laptop Bill"

Information Master 17

Placards 17A–17G

Placard 17D: One House Votes "Yes" on the "Laptop Bill"

Placard 17F: The Other House Votes "Yes" on the "Laptop Bill"

Placard 17B: The Governor Signs the "Laptop Bill"

Placard 17E: The "Laptop Law" Goes Into Effect

If the two teams hold up different sequences, help students figure out the correct sequence. Close the discussion with a summary of the correct order of steps. (**Note:** You may wish to have students open their Student Editions to Section 17.6 and study the diagram at this point.)

Phase 2: Conducting Research on State Government

4 **Prepare for Phase 2 of the activity.** Make enough copies of *Student Handout 17A: Researching Your State's Government* and *Student Handout 17B: Writing a Letter to a State Leader* to give one copy to each student. (**Note:** You may wish to provide some research resources in class or provide time outside of class to do research.)

5 **Have students research details about your state's government.** Distribute Student Handout 17A to students. Give students an adequate amount of time to complete their research and answer the questions.

6 **Have students write a letter to a state leader.** Distribute Student Handout 17B to students. Review the directions and have students complete the writing activity.

7 **Ask volunteers to share their letters.** After students read their letters, direct them to assume the roles of legislators and vote to approve or reject the proposed law. Discuss the outcome. (**Note:** If you want to send a letter to a legislator, have students vote on which one to send.)

Reading Further: Student Citizens Help Make a Law

1 **Prepare for the Reading Further activity.** Before the class, write to your state legislature and request a petition form. Divide students into mixed ability groups of four. Make enough copies of the petition to give each group one copy.

2 **Project** *Transparency 17: The Legislative Process.* Ask the following visual discovery questions to review with students how laws are made:

- What does this chart show?

- What steps does a bill follow before it becomes a law?

3 **Explain that this chart shows how laws are made in most states.** Tell students that they are going to read about a group of students who participated in the legislative process of turning an idea into a bill and then into a law.

4 **Have students read Reading Further 17 in their Student Editions.** Allow them to read independently or in small groups.

Reading Strategy: Create a Flow Chart

Review with students the idea of a flow chart, in which a diagram is used to show the step-by-step process of how something works. Have them create a flow chart of the legislative process based on their experience in the game. They can use the chart for reference when they write their letters.

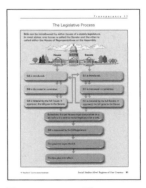

Student Handouts 17A and 17B

Transparency 17

5 To help students understand the right of free petition, have them under-take the process themselves.

- Distribute one copy of the petition form to each group of four. Explain that these are real petitions from your state's legislature. Discuss the petition with the class. Ask: *What do you think when you look at this petition? Is it what you expected a petition to look like or not? Why?*

- Ask students to open their Interactive Student Notebooks to Reading Further 17. Discuss the directions and clarify any questions.

- After students have created their own lists of possible new state symbols, create a class list on the board or on chart paper. Vote on the possibilities and choose one symbol.

- Option: Fill out a petition with your class for the winning idea and submit it to a state representative for consideration.

Assessment

Masters for the chapter assessment appear in the *Lesson Masters*. Answers appear below.

Big Ideas

1. C	4. D	7. C
2. A	5. D	8. A
3. B	6. B	

Social Studies Skills

9. Governor signs bill

10. legislative branch

11. to discuss the bill

12. The governor can choose to sign or veto a bill passed by the legislature.

13. Possible answer: How a Bill Becomes a Law

Show You Know

14. The bulleted points can serve as a rubric for this item.

English Language Learners

Simplify the writing requirements for students by putting them in a group so that the tasks can be subdivided. Modify the requirements for the letter or guide students, as needed, with additional structure, such as "Write two or more sentences to introduce and describe the problem. Include two or more sentences that describe what you want your leader to do."

Students with Special Needs

During the *How an Idea Becomes a Law* game, ask students questions and reiterate information to reinforce comprehension. The added structure will assist them in writing their letters. You can also provide sample letters for them to read and study before and during the writing of their own letters.

Enrichment

Have students create if-then flow charts to illustrate the process of how a citizen's idea can become a law, with different paths resulting from different options. For example, if a bill is sponsored by a state senator, the flow chart leads in one direction, but if it isn't, the flow chart leads in another. Students might use a software program to create their flow charts electronically. The completed flow charts can be used to help classmates review the process of how a bill becomes a law in their state.

Enrichment Resources

LearnTCI

Have students find out more about state government by exploring the following Enrichment Resources for *Social Studies Alive! Regions of Our Country*, at www.learntci.com.

Internet Connections These recommended Web sites provide useful and engaging content that enforces skills development and mastery of subjects within the chapter.

Enrichment Readings These in-depth readings encourage students to explore selected topics related to the chapter. You may also find readings that relate the chapter's content directly to your state's curriculum.

TeachTCI

For the teachers' resources listed below, click on Enrichment Resources for *Social Studies Alive! Regions of Our Country* at www.teachtci.com.

Biography Bank Hundreds of short biographies of notable people in history are available in PDF format for you to share with your students.

***Study Your State* Resources** Teaching directions and student activity pages (PDF format) will help you guide your students through researching their state.

Additional Reading Opportunities

The following nonfiction books offer opportunities to extend the content in this chapter.

Government: How Local, State, and Federal Government Works by Mark Friedman (Chanhassen, MN: The Child's World, Inc., 2005)
Students learn how people make changes in local, state, and national government by serving as elected officials. The branches of government on each level are also discussed.

What Are the Parts of Government? by William David Thomas (Pleasantville, NY: Gareth Stevens Publishing, 2008)
Students learn about the three branches of government and how they function. This book is part of the *My American Government* series. Titles include *How Do We Elect Our Leaders?*, *What Are Citizens' Basic Rights?*, and *What Is a Constitution?*

Read Sections 17.2 through 17.7, and record answers to the questions below.

17.2 Who shares power in a federal system of government?

The federal government and the state government share power.

17.3 What are the three branches of government, and what does each branch do?

The three branches of government are the legislative branch, the executive branch and the judicial branch. The legislative branch writes laws. The executive branch carries out the laws. The judicial branch makes sure people are treated with fairness.

17.4 Why are leaders important in a republic?

In a republic, people choose leaders to act for them.

17.5 How do we choose our leaders?

We choose leaders by voting for them.

17.6 How does an idea become a state law?

First, citizens must get enough support for the idea to convince a state legislator to write a bill. The legislature then debates and votes on the bill. If they approve the bill, it goes to the governor. If the governor signs the bill, it becomes a law.

17.7 Give one or more examples of citizen rights. Give one or more examples of citizen responsibilities.

Citizen rights include the right to vote and the right to free speech. Citizen responsibilities include voting, paying taxes, serving on a jury, obeying laws, respecting others' rights, and developing leadership traits.

	1	2	3	4	5	6	7	8	9	10	11	12	13	14	15	16	17
Map and Globe Skills																	
Recognize maps and globes as models		•		•		•	•	•		•		•					
Use map tools		•															
Directions/compass rose		•															
Symbols		•															
Legend		•															
Scale		•															
Identify locations		•															
Relative (spatial relationships, orientation)		•															
Absolute (alpha-numeric grid, latitude and longitude)		•															
Use different types of maps		•															
Map projections																	
Physical maps		•															
Political maps		•															
Special purpose maps		•															
Citizenship and Participation Skills																	
Respect American heritage			•	•													•
Recognize rights and responsibilities of citizenship																	•
Participate in groups	•	•											•			•	
Respect points of view			•														
Assume leader and follower roles													•			•	
Resolve conflicts													•			•	

	1	2	3	4	5	6	7	8	9	10	11	12	13	14	15	16	17
Graphic and Visual Skills																	
Interpret graphic information									•			•					
Graphs									•			•					
Charts									•								
Tables																	
Diagrams																•	
Timelines	•																
Analyze photographs and other images	•	•	•	•	•	•	•	•	•	•	•	•	•	•	•	•	•
Critical Thinking Skills																	
Classify	•																
Compare and contrast		•	•		•				•								
Sequence									•				•		•		
Cause and effect	•				•		•		•		•						
Analyze	•				•				•								
Distinguish fact and opinion	•																
Evaluate					•		•										
Draw conclusions					•		•										
Make inferences									•								
Generalize														•	•	•	•
Predict							•										
Make decisions																	•
Solve problems													•		•		
Identify point of view	•		•						•								
Analyze primary and secondary sources	•														•		
Recognize bias and propaganda																	
Support a position									•								

	1	2	3	4	5	6	7	8	9	10	11	12	13	14	15	16	17
Reading/Language Arts and Study Skills																	
Apply social studies content reading skills	•	•	•	•	•	•	•	•	•	•	•	•	•	•	•	•	•
Use expository text features	•	•	•	•	•	•	•	•	•	•	•	•	•	•	•	•	•
Identify main idea and details				•		•		•		•		•			•		•
Summarize				•		•		•		•		•			•		•
Ask and answer questions	•	•	•	•	•	•	•	•	•	•	•	•	•	•	•	•	•
Develop vocabulary	•	•	•	•	•	•	•	•	•	•	•	•	•	•	•	•	•
Write for a variety of social studies purposes				•		•		•		•		•			•		•
Listen to acquire information				•		•		•		•		•					
Use speaking skills to communicate effectively	•												•		•		
Conduct research														•	•	•	•
Locate, organize, analyze, and evaluate resources (print, electronic, oral)														•	•	•	•

Lesson Guide

Photographs
Cover
David Olsen/Getty Images

Title Page
David Olsen/Getty Images

Art

34 C: Susan Jaekel **34 TR:** Doug Roy **34 BR:** Renate Lohmann **34 TL:** Siri Weber Feeney **34 BL:** Len Ebert **48:** DJ Simison **50:** DJ Simison **60:** Doug Roy **61:** Doug Roy **62:** Doug Roy **72:** DJ Simison **74:** DJ Simison **82:** Doug Roy **84:** Doug Roy **97:** DJ Simison **99:** DJ Simison **112:** DJ Simison **114:** DJ Simison **116:** DJ Simison **127:** DJ Simison **129:** DJ Simison **158:** DJ Simison **160:** DJ Simison **179:** Doug Roy **190:** Doug Roy **201:** Gary Undercuffler

Artists represented by Ann Remen-Willis, Artist Representative and Art Manager:
Len Ebert
Susan Jaekel
Renate Lohmann
Doug Roy
DJ Simison
Gary Undercuffler
Siri Weber Feeney

Placards

Photographs
Chapter 7
12: Kent F. Berg/The Miami Herald/Getty Images

Chapter 9
13: Culver Pictures **14:** Brown Brothers **15:** Brown Brothers **16:** Culver Pictures **17:** Brown Brothers **18:** Brown Brothers **19:** Culver Pictures **20:** Minnesota Historical Society/Corbis **21:** Hulton-Deutsch Collection/Corbis

Art

22: Len Ebert **23:** Len Ebert **24:** Len Ebert **25:** Len Ebert **26:** Len Ebert **27:** Len Ebert **28:** Len Ebert **29:** Len Ebert **30:** Len Ebert **31:** Len Ebert **32:** Len Ebert **33:** Len Ebert **34:** Len Ebert **35:** Len Ebert

Artists represented by Ann Remen-Willis,
Artist Representative and Art Manager:
Len Ebert